*To friends in France and elsewhere, researchers, the military,
aircraft and helicopter pilots, to national and non-governmental
organizations, all of whom contributed, in ways great and small,
to the success of my expeditions in the bush.
To my family, who supported me through difficult times.
To our guardian angels, to all those who watch over us on our paths.*

secret jungle

Nicole Viloteau

Flammarion

My fascination with reptiles and nature's beauty goes back to my childhood in the Morvan region of France, where I explored the meadows and woods in search of flowers and animals. I have always been amazed by the bright and delicate colors of tropical forests. After more than twenty-five years of studying in the field (Africa, Asia, Australia, South America, Madagascar), I have seen the beauty and usefulness of forests throughout the world, and the urgency of preserving them before it's too late. Each and every minute, 75 acres (30 hectares) of virgin forest disappear from the earth.

All of the photographs in this book revive memories and emotions for me. Which has the strongest impact on me? The eyes of animals flushed out in the evening, in the middle of the night, or at dawn. Animals trapped by poachers and those dead from parasitosis. Other images, bursting with bright colors, stimulate me when I'm tired. Over the years, I have learned about the superb and implacable order that governs Nature. My multiple adventures in solitary bivouacs and reckless quests are inextricably linked to both fear and caution. Surviving under extreme conditions required an excellent physical condition based on an in-depth knowledge of the milieu I was exploring: dense forests, swampy areas, mangroves and savannas with gallery-forests. A respectful approach to the ethnic groups that live in harmony with the bush (Pygmies, Indians, aborigines) has always provided me with a rich source of information (language, traditional medicine).

Exploring is also a personal battle; it means pushing yourself to the limit, to discover and overcome your weaknesses – to learn without interfering or destroying! Fear and wonder are part and parcel of the trip. I have often been tempted to turn back and give up the fight. Then suddenly, something unexpected happens to change my mind: a bright blue butterfly appears, as if to remind me of my task. I forget my fatigue and devote myself to new photographs of these treasures enclosed in the forest. One full-moon night in the Ivory Coast, while I was listening, intrigued, to the distant sound of howling chimpanzees, a six-horned apple-green snail slid down my cheek: the mystery and charm of this wide-awake world bombards the senses at every moment.

Page 6: hairy violets. Tropical rainforest on the eastern seaboard of North Queensland.
Page 7: Gold Coast jungle, Queensland, Australia.
Above: Drosera indica, a carnivorous plant. Australia.
Facing page: tropical rainforest, Hinchinbrook Island, North Queensland.

11:30 P.M. I am writing in my tent, under the light on my head lamp. Nearby I hear the Pacific Ocean roaring in the dark. A storm thunders somewhere behind the mountains. A torrential rain pelts down on the forest, spattering on the fabric of the tent. I take advantage of a break in the weather to record the ambient noise with a small pocket recorder. All around, the jungle is dripping. Giant tree frogs are in full cry in the tree tops. There's a din of painted chubby frogs in a nearby swamp, and squeaks from mole-crickets. A green star pulsates over my head. A firefly! It's after midnight, jungle-time, according to my compass-watch. Tonight, the Southern Cross is nowhere to be seen. The jungle undergoes a metamorphosis as the hours pass. Sheets of phosphorus shine on the ground. Billions of microscopic fungi illuminate the dead leaves and tree trunks, creating a magical nighttime extravaganza. After the storm, the forest floor exudes a strong scent of vinegar, ether and rotting plants. Seeds burst open in the air, spiraling downward to the ground. Through the netting I spot clouds of mosquitoes standing guard. A greenish moon appears from behind the wide round leaves of a fan-palm, casting bluish sheen over the foliage and reflecting puddles. 6 A.M. The gray light of dawn. A chorus of birds in song. The jungle awakens. I savor the hot tea in my Thermos bottle, eat a large bowl of cereal and nibble on some dried fruit. I'm ready. A new day is about to begin, filled with the promise of exciting discoveries. I take off once again, my backpack heavy with all my gear and camera equipment. Walking through nature is like reinventing a dance step with perpetually new elements.

dawn of the world

On the tree of life, if mammals form the main branch,
primates are shoots off this branch
and hominoids the bud at the end of the shoot.
After millions of years growing under the horizon
in a single, highly localized spot, a flame shall burst forth.
Thought is here.

Teilhard de Chardin, *Phénomène humain*

The earth, which is more than 4.5 billion years old, has undergone the most dramatically violent geological and climatic upheavals: volcanic eruptions, ice ages, and continental drift — to name but a few. Today, veritable living fossils from these prehistoric periods still exist on a few of the Lesser Sunda Islands (Nusa). For example, on Komodo Island there are dragons 11 1/2 feet (3.5 meters) tall, weighing 350 pounds (160 kg), which are related to the great dinosaurs and tyrannosaurus from the Jurassic period.

Some 430 million years ago, plants covered the earth's landmass. These included tree ferns, giant moss, and lichen. The first flowers appeared around 200 million years ago, while the first fruit (*Archaefructus*) flourished around 140 million years ago. Unfortunately, only a few isolated traces of this shrinking paleoforest subsist around the world. These primary forests, easier to penetrate than secondary forests, are overgrown with valuable species and even arbor extremely rare "tree-relics." They are home to highly diverse fauna, a challenge to uncover. These damp crypts, cathedrals of green, where the canopy lets only two to five percent of the sun's rays filter through, are enchanted lands for the naturalist in the field.

Morning mist rising over Mount Todoklea on the volcanic Sunda Islands in Indonesia. I spent two months here in 1991, studying the behavior of the Komodo Dragons in their various biotopes: high-altitude jungles, forested savannas, monsoon forests. Being able to approach them so closely was a unique adventure.

High-altitude jungle north of Mount Bowen (3,609 feet/1,100 meters), January, February, 1983. Hinchinbrook (or Injun-Borr-Roo) Island, North Queensland, Australia.

This large island, a national park with a surface area of nearly 100,000 acres (39,350 hectares), is 260 million years old. In the foreground, a carpet of yellowish bushes (*Borya septentrionalis*) and primitive ferns (*Bowenia sp.*). I explored the most remote mountainous areas on the island (Mount Diamantina, Mount Straloch), which are riddled with potential dangers: landslide areas, vertiginous cliff tops, rivers raging after torrential rainfalls, and poisonous ticks. Yet these areas also harbor primitive plants that exist nowhere else in the world, and caves glittering with pure quartz crystal.

Sakaleona Falls (656 feet/200 meters). Tanala country, south Madagascar. A wall of roaring water, hard to reach. It took twelve days to walk the 120 miles (200 km) through this land ridden with obstacles. Endless river crossings, swamps, rice paddies, precarious bridges, climbs and descents before reaching this sublime destination. We were lucky to be only the second expedition to reach this remote spot in 1989. The rocky output, sticky with algae and giant moss, is carpeted with carnivorous plants. Beaded with deadly nectar, these creeping green plants trap insects. Below, on a hillside, a tiny village of Tanala woodsmen. The jungle is essential to the planet's equilibrium. It gives off thousands of tons of water each year. This evaporation results in torrential rains, which feed into streams and rivers. Excessive deforestation and increasing population in the twentieth century are responsible for dramatic worldwide water shortages: today, one in five people do not have drinking water, and the current reserves are insufficient.

Rain forest with elegant palm trees (*Ptychosperma elegans*), alexander palms (*Archontophoenix alexandra*), cabbage palms (*Livistona drudii*) and primitive black palm trees, relics from the paleoforest. Brook Island in the Great Barrier Reef, North Queensland, Australia. **Rain forest** with fan palms (*Licuala ramsayi*) and climbing palm trees (*Calamus moti*). Hinchinbrook Island, North Queensland, Australia. I hear the roar of the Pacific Ocean. White coral beaches and shells. There's no one here! I feel like I'm on Robinson Crusoe's island. I hear the muted cooing of the white pigeons from Torres, who nest here, far from any trigger-happy hunters. A green and bordeaux-colored woopoo pigeon screeches from the top of a primitive black palm tree. Elsewhere, a drongo with satiny-black feathers and ruby-red eyes produces a three-tone cluck. An iridescent green catbird mewls up and down the scale, then takes flight behind a royal palm tree. This is a paradise for birds. Motionless, I listen to the forest sing: a green bubble, looking like a stained-glass window, fragrant with cumin, cloves, and all sorts of indescribable, heady scents.

This sprouting young fern looks like a green scepter, unwinding its sap- and chlorophyll-filled stem. Only just out of the ground, it already has to fight against other plants blocking the light it needs to grow. With water and carbonic gas, plants convert solar energy into organic material through the process of photosynthesis. Mission Beach Rain Forest, North Queensland, Australia.
Green tree snake (*Elaphe oxycephala*). Java, Indonesia. In the Garden of Eden, did the serpent – the source of original sin – look like this? A seductive creature, it slithers along and stops, immobile, against a backdrop of leaves that blend with its skin. Its blue, Y-shaped tongue seems to mock the heavens.

African nutmeg flower (*Monodora myristica*).
Virgin forest near Mount Iboundji, Gabon.
The forest discloses its mysteries in tiny increments.
The sacred is revealed, in time, through constant
walking, effort, and fear. Flowers often repeat
symbolic shapes as they bloom: the reversed double
triangulation of these petals expresses a
mathematical truth.
"When you wake up in the morning, give thanks
for the light of day, for your life and your strength.
Give thanks for food and happiness. If you see no
reason to give thanks, the fault lies within you."
Tecumseh, Shawnee Indian chief, 1768–1813.
The end of the world? Trees explode like bombs, as
columns of green flames lick the trunks of eucalyptus
trees, which collapse in the cacophony of a storm and
whirlwinds of orange cinders. A multitude of wild animals are burned alive in this roaring inferno. Clouds
of burning grasshoppers flee the deluge of fire.
Falcons pounce on the dying and fleeing animals.
I am suffocating in the flames, and race toward the
last breach of untouched forest. Safe from the fire,
I watch this ecological disaster helplessly. Each year
in Australia and throughout the world, criminally set
fires ravage thousands of acres of forests.
Cape York Peninsula, North Queensland, Australia.

immersion

*But one of the great things, far more exciting than going
to the moon, would have been not Darwin, but Captain Cook.
On his first and second voyage, he went round the Pacific
and went to Tahiti where he saw a new brand of humanity,
and a completely new set of animals and plants.
That must have been mind-blowing. The reverse side of the coin
in having this extraordinary ability to go anywhere,
is that no-one anywhere is remote any more. I just caught
the end of it in the mid-fifties. When I was right in the middle
of Borneo, you thought you were in a different world.
There was no radio, no ways of communicating – but
it was nothing compared to what Cook did. I just wish
the world was twice as big and half of it was still unexplored.*

David Attenborough

July 1996. A forestry site near Yombi, in southwest Gabon. I put up my tent in a gallery-forest overlooking a lake encircled by dense vegetation. Each day, from dawn to dusk, I explore my surroundings looking for animals and flowers to photograph. I take a short-cut through a small savanna dense with guava trees laden with ripe fruit. I stand there and stuff myself, then fill my pockets for the rest of the day. A drum roll, followed by peals of laughter, catches my attention. A large, yellow-beaked blue touraco looks down at me from the top of a wild atangatier with small, edible mauve fruit. I take a break at the base of an Okoumé tree. Translucent green resin drips down the wounded trunk. I gather a few drops on a rolled-up leaf and inhale the powerful scent, which reminds me of both incense and turpentine. Sprinkling a bit on hot coals keeps mosquitoes away. It's 86° F (30° C) at the edge of the forest. Someone is walking behind me. I'm frightened – it's a gorilla! An old gray male. Greatly relieved, I watch as he disappears into the depths of the undergrowth.

Preceding pages:
Virgin forest, Wongua-Wongué, Gabon. The virgin forest stretches upward over four levels. On the ground are mosses, lichens, and dwarf ferns. Higher up are shrubs, grasses, and trees of varying heights. In Gabon, the silk-cotton tree grows to 130 feet (70 meters). This forest is haunted by gorillas, chimpazees, and assalas, which are small elephants.
Virgin forest, Woleu-Ntem, Gabon. Dark and dense, the primary forest is easier to explore than a secondary forest, which is protected by inextricable walls of plants. Indeed, the small amount of light filtering through the canopy hinders the growth of herbaceous plants.

Swamps and flooded forests in the region of Lastourville, Gabon. The drowned trees creak and crack, whipped around by winds and storms. These columns of bone-dry tree trunks, evoke baroque palaces or acropolises in ruin. Panthers, elephants, buffaloes, warthogs, and clouds of multi-colored butterflies come here to drink. At night, the trees and branches are illuminated with wreaths of incandescent eyes: tree frogs, galagos, and damans. Crocodiles splash through the silt. Sometimes, a phosphorescent ballet of courting fireflies enlivens this swampy tomb of dead trees, which is quickly recycled by detrivores.

A wall of climbing ferns in a mountainous forest.
A constant flow of spring water has worn cracks in the
rocks; the rippling noise is accompanied by the croaking
of frogs. It's wonderful to scoop such pure water up in
your hands when you're so exhausted. Mount Bartle
Frère, Tableland, North Queensland. Australia.
Annual rainfall: 150 to 200 inches (4,000 to
5,000 mm) in the Tully region.
Boyd's forest dragon (*Gonocephalus boydii*),
24 inches (60 cm). Extremely rare. Indigenous to the Tully
region, this small aquatic and tree-dwelling reptile feeds
on insects and mollusks. North Queensland, Australia.

Young cassowary (*Casuarius casuarius*), caught by
surprise at the edge of the jungle. North Queensland,
Australia. Seventy species of trees depend on the
cassowary: the seeds must pass through the digestive
system of the cassowary before they can germinate. This
aggressive animal is related to the ostrich and measures
5 to 6 feet (1.50 to 1.80 meters). It is a wingless bird, but
can run as fast as 30 mph (50 kph) in case of danger.
If the cassowary wore shoes they would be a size 7 (37)!
Its stabbing claw is 5 inches (12 cm) long and can
disembowel an enemy. Its warning cry is a frightening,
guttural "boom-boom."

A forest of giant lichen and moss, home to *Nepenthes
madagascariensis*, carnivorous tropical pitcher plants. Their
pitchers give off a heavy scent of crushed daisies and
musk. The poor butterflies and lizards don't have a chance.
Once they've fallen for the trap, it takes just a few days
before they have been completely dissolved and absorbed.

A **curtain of liana**, genus *Tetrastigma,* "Matchbox," and other *Cordylines. Ptychosperma* palms, *Hoya* epiphytes. Lake Eacham, Tableland, North Queensland, Australia. All types of liana flourish in tropical forests. Some contain drinkable water, others a fearsome poison (strychnine, cyanide or prussic acid). In Gabon, the *Strophantus glabrus,* with superb pink flowers and a noxious scent, produces seeds that are highly poisonous.

A **band of brown lemurs** moves noisily through the trees looking for wild flowers and fruit. They also love eggs, fledglings, snails, and insects. This female brown lemur (*Lemur fulvus*) carrying her young has spotted a giant iule; she captures the myriapod between her black-skinned palms and crunches into it. An orange liquid drips out between her teeth. Her fellow creatures can leap up to 20 feet (6 meters); they greedily eat my last bananas. Certain lemurs, when threatened, secrete a repellent liquid that is extremely nauseating and tenacious. Males mark their territory with their scrotal scent glands and those on their forearms. Females use their musk-scented vulvar glands to imbue leaves and branches along their paths.

Tanala woodsman. Region near Sakaleona Falls, southwest Madagascar. This small ethnic group lives in an enclave of the mountain jungle. Its members know all about the virtues of plants and use them in their traditional medicine. "Next to a plant that kills can be found its antidote," goes a popular saying. In the words of an elder: "You have to be aware of what you receive from a tree you encounter: soothing shade under which you can rest, edible fruit, fallen branches for a fire, fragrant flowers to help you relax and which heal all sorts of illnesses."

A giant braided liana. Rain forest in North Queensland, Australia. Making your way through the jungle is a discipline that takes time to master. Nature sets the rules, not man. This is not the place for daring athletic feats. Nature teaches a respect for its obstacles and the art of bypassing them and even putting them to good use. Your body must adapt to all the various elements. A passage always exists wherever you are, if you know how to look for it: an animal track; a gorge through the rocks; supple liana used as rappel lines; and fallen trees spanning rivers, ravines or unapproachable labyrinths of plants (brambles, giant nettles, stinging liana). The jungle is the best training ground for athletes that exists: you have to be extremely vigilant and ready to go through all sorts of contortions to explore it and survive under the extreme conditions. You have to constantly stay alert and make optimal use of all of your physical, intellectual, and extra-sensorial aptitudes: climbing, crawling, scaling, somersaulting, sliding, and jumping. It's an exhilarating hand-to-hand battle.

A Bamboo forest and fisherman in a monoxyl dugout canoe. Sambirano, Madagascar. The key to survival: when you get lost in a dense forest, remember that springs lead to streams and to rivers, hence to civilization. The quantity of fresh water in the world represents only 3 percent of the total volume of water on the planet; 1 percent is used for consumption by man (the other 2 percent is used for agricultural purposes – a disturbingly high amount).

A ritual statue in Papua New Guinea. In Oceania, as elsewhere in the world, primitive ethnic groups honor the cult of forest spirits in the form of statuettes and totems to which they make offerings. Certain groups practice votive sacrifices to ward off evil spirits and to ensure prosperity and fertility for the villagers.

I-oh-uuu-oh-i-oh-uu!
What is this yodeling coming out of the deep forest? It's the Aka Pygmies of Bokoka, also called the "small singing men": they sing constantly, from morning to night, as they go about their day. These nomadic hunters and gatherers trade honey and wild-animal meat for large sacks of salt, which they consider as valuable as gold.
Left: an Aka hunter-gatherer (Lower Lobaye, Central African Republic, 1978), with his crossbow and sheath of poison darts.
Right: an Aka Pygmy walking in front of his round hut made of branches and intertwined leaves of marantacee. *Kemu vite mandjogho mutu a tsinga vite ikoulou* (The monkey follows the trees; man, the hut). An Eshira proverb, Gabon, noted by Adrien Mbouma (*The Voice of the Ancestors*).

A paleoforest containing primitive old beech trees (*Nothofagus*) and "grass trees" (*Xanthorrea sp.*), which form large tufts of hard grasses that could poke out the eye of an absent-minded or nocturnal explorer. They grow only 4 inches (10 cm) per century. Volcanic mountains (rhyolite and trachyte), Macpherson Range, New South Wales, Australia. The "mystery bird," a pretty black-and-white shrike with a lovely voice, also lives in this remote area. **Old Tiger,** an aborigine elder from the Arnhem Lands, in Black Point on the Coburg Peninsula. North Territory, Australia. In 1983, I was invited by the Dhuwa and Yirritja aborigines to spend three and a half months with them, to teach about serpents and how to treat snakebites; in exchange, they shared their knowledge of traditional medicinal plants.

harmonious geometry

Even in places where the human spirit seems completely at liberty to give free reign to its creative spontaneity, there is neither disorder nor whimsy in the choice of images made, or in the way they are associated, opposed, or linked.

Claude Lévi-Strauss

I am amazed at the architectural magnificence of tropical rain forests. At first site they may appear to be uniform, but step by step, you discover plants that grow in perfect geometric shapes. Liana, tree ferns, palm trees, giant moss, roots, trunks, but also branches, leaves, and flowers illustrate the prodigious unity of the entire forest, a harmony that appears to have been marvelously planned by nature: the pictorial triumph of Gothic arches created by foliage; flying buttresses of climbing roots; and creeping "pipelines" of roots. Most plants have a repetitive geometry due to axial or bilateral symmetry. Some of their structures are spiral-shaped. Brimming with plant and animal species of indescribable colors, nature is a constant source of inspiration for both photographers and for painters.

Preceding page:
Ferns and palm tree (*Pandanus*). North Queensland, Australia.
A green tree snake (*Gastropyxis smaragdina*) slithers to a stop on a branch of raffia palm. Mondah Forest, Gabon. It is monochromic and homotypic, which provides a highly effective camouflage; the snake can see without being seen, making it easier to flee a predator or capture prey. This tree snake eats chameleons, geckos, and small birds. In Antiquity, Aesculapius' snake symbolized medicine (in the form of the caduceus). Shortly after I captured this snake, I crossed paths with a *nganga* (native healer), carrying all sorts of medicinal plants in her raffia basket. Given my deep-rooted passion for snakes, she took me for a magician. In the shadow of her hut, she read my future in seeds tossed onto a panther skin surrounded by burning candles.

Thorny liana (*Calamus sp.*) Rain forest, North Queenland, Australia. The walls of supple liana are hellish for a photographer: backpacks get stuck in them and they scratch your hands, face, and wrists. The thorns are so thin in the shadowy green undergrowth that they are virtually invisible. If a magnificent butterfly appears directly behind them, the fascinating apparition can make you forget these sharp barbs barring the path. The consequences are immediate: sharp pain and drops of blood. Aborigines use this liana for fishing lines and to suture wounds.

A two-horned Madagascar chameleon (*Calummo nasuta*) on a fragrant leaf (*Aframumum sp.*). A tree-climber, thanks to its prehensile tail and gripping legs, this small, 10-inch (25-cm) lizard changes color depending on its moods, the heat, the humidity, and its state of health. Four layers of pigments (melanophore, allophore, lipophore, and guanophore) in the animal's epidermis and dermis are responsible for the chameleon's ability to change colors.

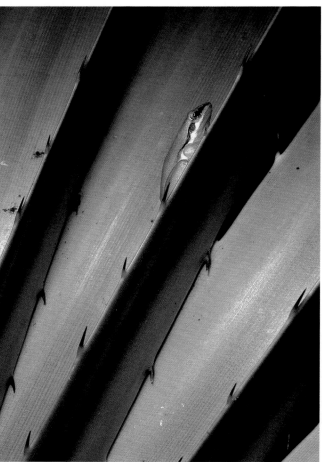

Northern dwarf tree frog (*Litoria bicolor*), 1/2 inch (1.5 cm) long, on *Pandamus* leaves. Black Mountains near Cooktown, North Queensland, Australia.
A chameleon (*Chamaeleo pardalis*) measuring 8 inches (20 cm) on a palm leaf. I saw this creature in the blink of an eye. Its eyes, which pivot front to back, had spotted a green fly on a viscous blue fruit. It flicked its tongue, but missed the target. When I captured it, it opened its mouth to bite me, at the same time turning an ugly dark brownish, neutral color. After petting its back, I took several photographs; it finally cooperated and gave me a few orange stripes – before I let it go again. Forest near Manakara, southeast Madagascar. There are 98 species of chameleons located in Africa and Asia.

Fragment of a tree fern. Triangulo Miniero relic forest, Minas Gerais, Brazil. Whether viewed in detail or as an ensemble, the tropical forest offers a thousand and one dreamscapes depending on the effects of the sun, moon, rain, and fog. The light is in constant movement. With each step, the forest offers a cathedral-like vision, with leaves forming puzzles of stained-glass patterns and translucent arches that change with the time of day and the season. This forest has been wiped off the map — cut down and burned out by lumber companies, the wildlife pillaged by poverty-ridden hunters. Farewell to the toucans, wolves, jaguars, monkeys, armadillos, anteaters, boas, and rattlesnakes. A number of factors contribute to the regression of tropical forests: cutting down trees for firewood or building materials, ground clearing for agriculture, and run-off of topsoil following torrential rains. Around the world, 75 acres (30 hectares) of virgin forest disappear every minute.

Palm leaf, Madagascar.
Green tree snake (*Elaphe oxycephala*). Java Jungle,
Indonesia. It's amazing how a snake can form hermetic
symbols and letters with its body as it slithers across tree
trunks and branches. Would this be "19" or perhaps
"Ω?"

I tripped over a root, bringing down several branches
as I fell; a green tree frog was asleep in one of them.
A comical encounter: startled, the frog opened its red
eyes wide. I caught it, then gently massaged its back
legs in a circular motion; it calmed down, allowing
me this portrait. Green tree frog (*Leptopelis sp*)
on a fingered leaf of an umbrella tree. Moss forest
of Tchimbélé, Crystal Mountains, Gabon.

Claws scratching and pathetic squeaks. I help out this unfortunate 2-inch (5-cm) rhinoceros beetle (*Oryctes nasicornis*), struggling on its back, wounded by the blinding light of a forestry lamp. These large nocturnal insects lay eggs in the roots of trees and eat the plant's sap. I keep my captive in a jar filled with leaves, then free him the next day, far from the deadly lights. Each year, millions of insects perish, victims of cities' bright lights. Mitzig, Gabon.

An armada of green ants (*Oecophylla smaragdina*) have taken over my camp, forming an incessant wave that sweeps over the tent roof. Where are they going? Direction: north-northwest. The following day, returning to the ranger's headquarters, I understand the reason for their flight: a bush fire is raging through the southern part of the reserve. We were all lucky to get out in time. For the aborigines, a massive flight of green ants is an early warning sign of an impending natural catastrophe: hurricane, flood, or bush fire. In case of danger, these aggressive ants spray formic acid on an intruder. Yet these are not the most fearsome of the ants; they do not devour humans, as do the ferocious marabuntas of South America or the manians of Africa.

It's nighttime. The bush is dripping wet after a rainfall; an elephant trumpets in the distance. A panther growls in a ravine. This is the time the Rhinoceros vipers (*Bitis nasicornis*) come out of the swampy depths. Their rough skin arrayed with uneven geometric patterns provides a perfect camouflage on the forest floor. Zomoko, Monts de Cristal Forest, Gabon.

Scales of an Australian marine crocodile tail (*Crocodylus porosus*). Cape York Peninsula, North Queensland. This is the longest species of crocodile in the world, up to 26 feet (8 meters). They are known to be man-eaters.

emerald jewels

The day has passed delightfully.
Delight itself, however, is a weak term
to express the feelings of a naturalist who,
for the first time, has wandered by himself
in a Brazilian forest. The elegance of
the grasses, the novelty of the parasitical
plants, the beauty of the flowers,
the glossy green of the foliage,
but above all the general luxuriance
of the vegeation, filled me with admiration.

Charles Darwin, *The Voyage of the Beagle*

August 1996. Forêt des Abeilles, Gabon. The sound of snorting, followed by strident cries, is moving closer. A troop of black monkeys is haranguing a family of red cercopithecus. Once they spot me, they all take off, disappearing into the dark bush. It's 80° F (27° C) in the shade. The sun has reached its zenith and strikes the hollow of a circular ravine, a meteorite crater filled with pink silt and inextricable vegetation. Bright reflections catch my eye. I climb down into the abyss, holding on to the branches of a giant tree that has fallen across it. Astonished, I discover cracked green quartz crystals with glints of purple forming a rainbow of colors. Others enclose khaki-colored herringbone patterns, pyramids of green moss, and vitrified landscapes of clay. I spend hours contemplating this treasure trove, open to the sky. Green tree frogs move through the strata of vegetation. A green cetonia flies heavily over the yellow-flowered shrubs. The equatorial rain forest conceals veritable gems matched to the leaves — animal, plant, and mineral are found in various shapes and textures and in every possible shade of green. But beware, some of the most attractive of these plants and animals can exude or inject the most dangerous of poisons!

58

The forest offers its treasures of sparkling colors in minute doses. Noisettes de Sorcière, toxic berries. Edge of the rain forest, North Queensland, Australia.
Micro-hylidae measuring 1 inch (2.5 cm). The frog's scent, like a rusty old tank, mixes with the noxious odor of this bunch of green fruit, fallen to the ground after a storm. Taï Forest, Ivory Coast, 1981.
A black night. Chimpanzees in the distance screech in terror. A reddish, gibbous moon rises over the mist-covered forest. Leaves move around my face. Something light, cold, and damp climbs up my cheek. I scream and yank it off. I turn on my head lamp and look at the ground. Amazed, I see a bright green snail waving its six horns at me. "Old folks like snails because they have no bones to trouble loose teeth." Gabonese proverb. Eshira tribe.Taï Forest, Ivory Coast, 1981.

Young fern. In just a few days, it will turn dark green. In this green Eden, seeds burst open after a rain; the young shoots battle each other toward the light. Palmerston National Park, North Queensland, Australia.
Christmas beetle. During the monsoon season, as Christmas nears, green beetles, 3/4 inch (2 cm), come by the hundreds from the forest, invading rangers' bungalows. *Eupecilia* is the most common genus in Australia.

Chameleon (*Chamaeleo pardalis*). Rain forest on the east coast, Antalaha region of Madagascar. The backs of some chameleons have bony, spiky scales. The rostral appendage is more pronounced in males than in females. During mating season, the males adopt spectacular colors. Their skins are dotted with colorful scales forming diverse patterns. This finery is intended to dissuade rivals.

A path through the virgin forest leads me up and down along vertiginous slopes and narrow curves with cascading torrents and waterfalls. Suddenly, a thin cord of shimmering green wriggles strangely at the base of a shrub. This unfortunate snake was mortally wounded by a falcon, which dropped it in mid-flight; after a few painful death throes, it lies motionless. I position it in a natural pose for a photograph and capture its beauty. Its gaping sides reveal flesh and blood; life has fled. Poisonous snake (*Dipsadoboa unicolor*). Monts de Cristal Forest, Gabon.

Symbol of fertility, power, and immortality, the serpent has been held sacred by many religions (ophidian cults). Note the feathered serpent, or Quetzacoatl, of the Aztecs; the Buddhists' sacred cobra; and Ouadjet, the Naja goddess, guardian of the Nile Delta.

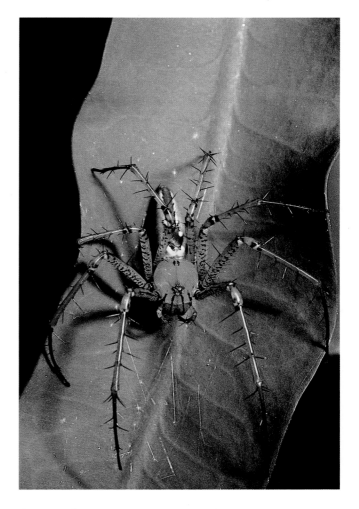

Green grasshopper measuring 1/2 inch (1.5 cm)
on a hibiscus flower. Gabon. Surrounded by a halo
of light pink in this inverted umbrella of silky
petals, a grasshopper remains safely concealed
from the eyes of winged predators.
A living trap of green chelicerae, this green
spider is well camouflaged on a leaf, where it sits
in wait for a careless fly or butterfly. Dry tropical
forest north of Port Berger, northwest Madagascar.
As opposed to insects, (which provide their daily
fare), spiders do not have faceted eyes, but a series
of eight eyes with crystalline lenses, to make
hunting easier by day or by night. Of the 20,000
known species of spiders in the world, only a
hundred or so are toxic — some deadly — to humans.

My little monster friend "Carolo," moves in fits and starts along an old reddish laterite track northwest of Farafangaina. As I take a photograph, he tries to escape, annoyed by my contortions — on my stomach, on all fours, or kneeling precariously off-balance. I scratch his back to calm him down. With mouth wide open, he rotates protruding eyes in every direction. Horned chameleon (*Chamaeleo willsii*). East Jungle, Madagascar.

With its scythe-like front pincers ready to strike, this green praying mantis kneels on a matching prie-dieu. Lying in ambush, it waits for an insect to come within reach. The female is a murderous lover; she often kills her mate during copulation, even while the male's sexual organ continues to function. Minas Gerais Forest, Brazil.

Sun shining through the leaf of a Rebecca fern.
Dunk Island, Australia. The forest spews a disturbing
blend of smells — mildew, potato flour, cumin, ether,
clove, vinegar, chocolate, violet, orange, and apricot.
Mountain jungle on Hinchinbrook Island, Australia.
Fan palms (*Licuala ramsayi* and *Licuala muellerii*) and
climbing palm, quandong with bright blue edible
fruit, red cedars, and Lilly-Pilly with red and white
apples that are fairly tasteless but rich in vitamins.
The Australian national parks now preserve 3 million
acres (1.2 million hectares) of tropical forests: it
occupies 0.3 percent of the continent's surface area
and stretches the length of the Sunshine Coast from
Townsville to the tip of Cape York.

Epiphytic plants with spiny, crenellated oblong leaves. Rain forest in North Queensland, Australia. **A grasshopper** cleaning itself up. This one has a rather unique feature: it's slightly cross-eyed. Secondary forest, El Arish, North Queensland, Australia.

In 1989, during a long expedition to the top of Tsaratanana (9,436 feet/2,876 meters), in northeast Madagascar, Tombo, one of our guides performed a traditional ritual: to ward off evil spirits, he had to release a white hen in the jungle. Shortly after, I discovered a spirit of benevolent places. This small chameleon, *Chamaeleo furcifer*, a champion climber (here on an interminable rubbery liana), lives a two-day walk from the summit.

A giant tree frog (*Litoria caerulea*) on a sacred lotus (*Nelumbo nucifera*), 14 inches (35 cm) in diameter, with leaves reaching up to 24 inches (60 cm) long. The lotus, like the frogs' legs, is edible. It's a risky undertaking to photograph the treasures of a swampy lagoon and not at all easy to reach this sacred pink lotus flower. I walk through water up to my chest, my boots sliding on a shifting bed of algae and underwater plants. Nevertheless, this cool, muddy dip is a relaxing break from the usual sweltering heat. Cape York Peninsula, Australia.

The yellow eye of an 11-1/2 foot (3.5-meter) green python (*Chondropython viridis*). Rare. Cape York Peninsula, Australia.

jungle mosaic

And the Lord God, planted a garden
eastward in Eden; and there he put
the man whom he had formed.
And out of the ground made the Lord God
to grow every tree that is pleasant
to the sight, and good for food;
the tree of life also in the midst
of the garden and the tree of knowledge
of good and evil. And a river went out
of Eden to water the garden . . .

Genesis II: 8–10

Pangalanes, east coast of Madagascar.
Two bees hum in a ray of sunshine. They land on the globular foliage, seeking pollen. Flowers discreetly hide. When they fall to the ground I discover perfect beauty with amazement. Shimmering, unsuspected colors brighten up the predominant green. Fruits, flowers, seeds, and tiny or microscopic creatures outdo one another in attractive shapes and colors, heady scents, digestive or mortally toxic chemical substances, with the unique aim of reproduction. Among insects, amphibians, reptiles, and birds, all kinds of finery, ruses, and disguises serve a dual purpose: sexuality and defense of their territory.

Today I walked 13 miles (22 km) over flat ground. On my way, I admired stalks of white orchids hanging from forked trees. Something moved along the forest floor strewn with fallen fruit. It was a magnificent vanilla yellow slug. Cutting across my path with slow, graceful movements, its iridescent wake of slime heightened the specter-like appearance. I stroked its back. Slimy and fearful, the slug transformed itself into a magical golden ring. Suddenly, the noise of human voices drew me out of my poetic musings. Yet there was no light in the forest. Were they stealing orchids? Trembling, I waited — a very long time!

Tropical and equatorial forests reveal all types of flora and fauna.
Page 77: Top left: *Banksia ericifolia* flowers. Laminghton Range, Queensland, Australia.
Top right: Toxic berry from a mangrove shrub. North Queensland, Australia.
Bottom left: Cauliflorous liana. Triangulo Miniero, Minas Gerais, Brazil.
Bottom right: Edible *Pandanus* fruit. Hinchinbrook Island, Australia.

Preceding double page:
A flower stalk coated with sticky nectar. This brightly colorful inflorescence reveals an extremely effective, whimsical sexuality: more than 95 percent of flowering plants simultaneously have both male (stamen) and female (pistil) characteristics. Forêt des Abeilles, Gabon.
Far left: **Wild currants.** Virgin forest near Koulamoutou, Gabon.
Above: **A tiny tree frog** (3/4 in./1.5 cm) (*Hyperolius sp.*) Racophoridae. Taï Forest, Ivory Coast.

Down on the ground and high up in the foliage
the monotony of ever-present green is broken by a
few rare sparks of bright color: flowers, fruits, seeds,
birds, reptiles, and frogs.
Far left, top: Barinda. Minas Gerais, Brazil.
Left, top: *Dillenia alata*, a flower, which blooms and
dies in a single night. Bamaga rain forest, North
Queensland, Australia.
Far left, bottom: *Hibiscus tilliaceus* flower. Mangrove
swamp on Hinchinbrook Island, Australia.
Left, bottom: Yellow lepiota, inedible mushrooms.
Fôret des Abeilles, Gabon.
Right: **Iule** *(Spirobolus sp.)* on the prickly fruit of a
liana. Virgin forest in north Gabon. Certain ethnic
groups capture this myriapod and use the brownish
liquid it secretes to disinfect wounds.

Green snake (*Elaphe oxycephala*) sloughing its skin.
The old skin or slough tears at the nose's end and
peels back like the finger of a glove as the snake
slithers and winds through the tree branches.
Java Island, Indonesia.
Young chameleon (*Chamaeleo sp.*) just after
sloughing its skin. Pangalanes, Madagascar.

A giant stick insect, 6 inches (14 cm) long. Mount Diamantina (2,952 feet/900 meters), Hinchinbrook Island, Australia. This insect is almost impossible to detect in its biotope of undergrowth.

Taking close-up photographs of a reptile requires an in-depth understanding of its biology, habits, and taxonomy — along with a large dose of patience for handling and to calm it down.

Right, top: Gabon chameleon (*Chamaeleo dilepis*). Its protruding eyes rotate independently, providing a wide view of its territory and making it easier to detect prey or an enemy.

Far right, top: Yellow stink bug. Gallery forest, Lakefield N.P., North Queensland, Australia.

Right, bottom: Yellow Nile monitor lizard (*Varanus niloticus*). Gabon. The uneven patterns of yellow and black keep this lizard safely camouflaged from its many predators: birds of prey, big cats, snakes, crocodiles, and even adults of its own species.

Far right, bottom: Indian monitor lizard (*Varanus indicus*). Bamaga Jungle, Top End of Cape York, Australia.

Young chondropython. Indonesia.
It's a scorcher! More than 104° F (40° C) at the
edge of the gallery-forest. The river has partly dried
up. Two dingoes drink quietly from a muddy puddle of
water. When they see me, they take off, frightened.
I've been exploring the sand and clay banks, which are
as hard as concrete, for hours. Something is making
ripples under the surface of the pond: a frog (*Litoria
nigrogrenata*) takes refuge on a stalk of a dried orchid.
Bamaga Jungle, Top End of Cape York, Australia.

It's **been a long**, exhausting hike. The heat is suffocating. The murmur of a spring draws me under a shady canopy. I swallow mouthfuls of pure water. Suddenly, an almost imperceptible movement attracts my attention. I turn and see a blue speck moving among the foliage.

The strange bird watches me, intrigued. It's a wren (*Malurus sp.*) with blue eyelids. Evening is approaching. Large red clouds cover part of the sky. Dry tropical forest of Ambohipaky, south of Soalala, west Madagascar.
Frilled-neck lizard (*Chlamydosaurus kingii*) in threatening posture. It is native to the bush and tropical rain forest of North Queensland, Australia.

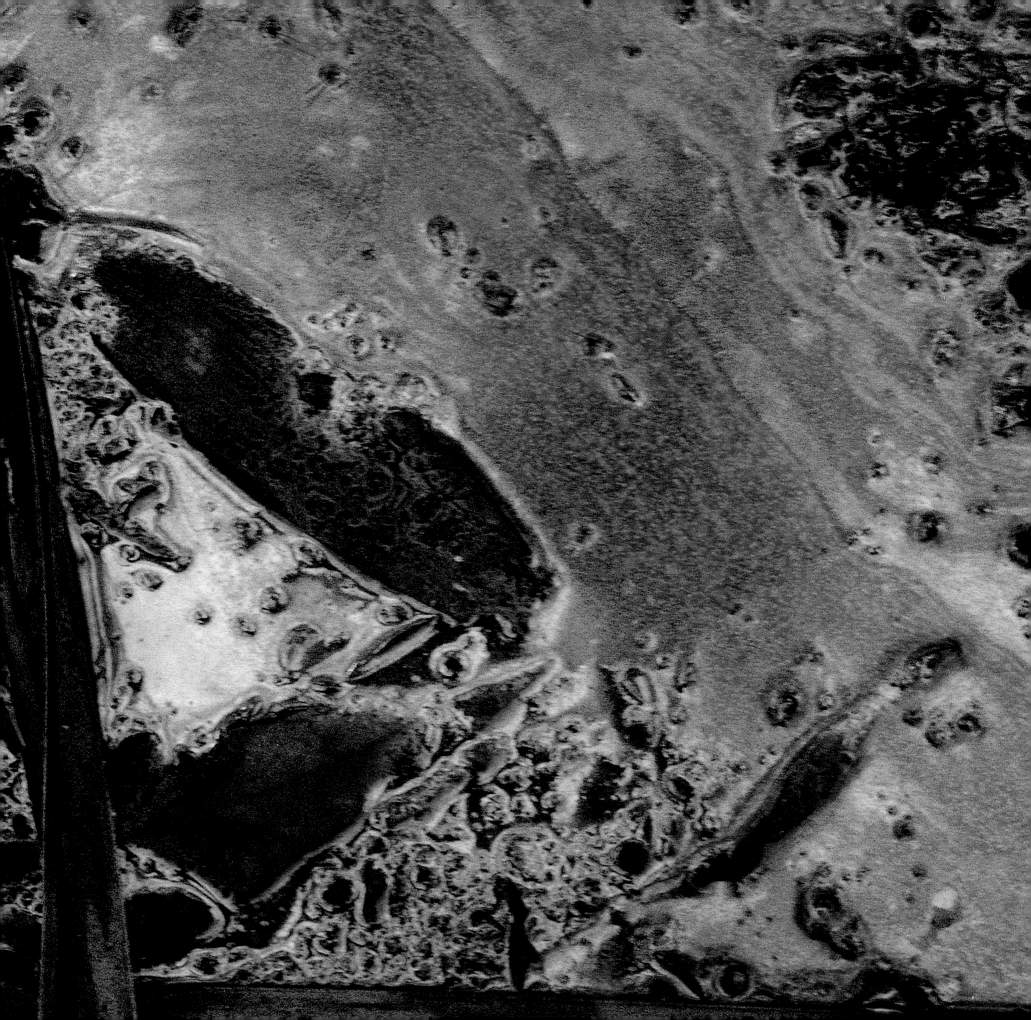

Is this an aerial view of the moon's surface? Or the reflection of a splintered, dull, and sticky rainbow? In fact, it's just a simple puddle of water, iridescent from the oil of rotting eucalyptus leaves. Heat and carbon dioxide accelerate the fermentation of plants. Galmara, forested region of North Cardwell, North Queensland, Australia.

Martian craters? Or the ritual cups of the shaman or sorcerer? These magical-looking blue pezizas have the consistency of cardboard. Lacking the chlorophyll they need for photosynthesis, the mushrooms obtain essential carbon by living as parasites on other plants.

An extremely rare blue python (*Chondropython viridis*). Indonesia. Decked out in turquoise scales, the python is coiled up in the fork of a tree branch, ready to unwind its loops to suffocate a prey.

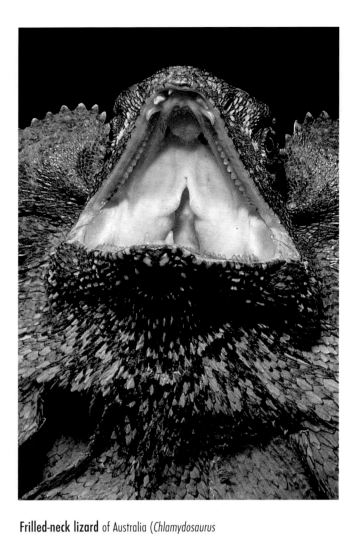

Frilled-neck lizard of Australia (*Chlamydosaurus Kingii*). Top end of Cape York Peninsula.
I'm lost. I've been walking a long time, looking for a source of water, a sign of human presence. I cross through a strange low forest of trees covered with moss and bearded lichen. In the distance, I hear a cock crow. The village rooster tells me which direction to head. Saved!
I encounter a turquoise-crested chameleon (*Chamaeleo cristatus*) near a manioc plantation, standing guard on a red padouk stump. The wood's characteristic color and the blood-red resin, smelling strongly of iodine, set off the lizard's small antediluvian shape. Monts de Cristal. North Gabon.

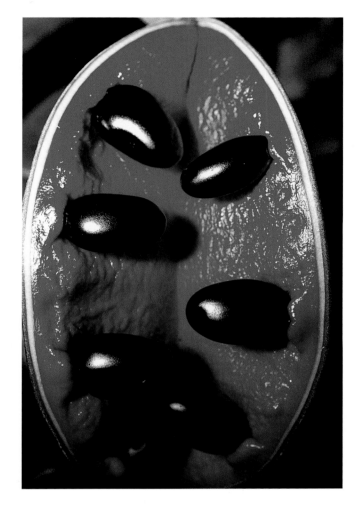

Red orchids. Rain forest, Thailand. This scorpion
orchid is of a most unusual color. Like all epiphytic
plants, orchids derive nutrients from host plants.
"If someone loves a flower, of which just one single
blossom grows in all the millions and millions of
stars, it is enough to make him happy just to look at
the stars. He can say to himself: 'My flower is there,
somewhere.' But if the sheep eats the flower, it's as
if all the stars have suddenly gone out." Antoine de
Saint-Exupéry, *The Little Prince.*
Have cockroaches infested a watermelon? No, this
is a giant open pod revealing its precious seeds.
Forêt des Abeilles, Gabon.

The forest is a cornucopia, truly offering its guests all the food and water necessary for survival.
Far left: Fruit from the tulip tree. Monts de Cristal, Gabon.
Left, top: This rare, eight-pointed mushroom grows on swampy ground. Laminghton Range, Australia.
Left, bottom: Red hygrophorus (*Hygrophorus sp.*), Virgin forest, Monts de Cristal, Gabon.
Right: **Australian mistletoe flowers** (*Amylotheca dictyophleba*). These extremely sticky, edible berries are not for fussy eaters! In the background, the dark chain of the Black Mountains (North Queensland), a hellish place of boulders covered with anthracite lichen. Black pythons and lizards haunt the unfathomable depths where, in the past, cowboys and their entire herds disappeared without a trace. Spiny shrubs, stinging trees, and choking fig trees block the entrance to this stone fortress. From the shadowy depths arise echoes, muffled wails, and the high-pitched song of the frogs. Some nights, rocks explode due to the extreme variation in temperature.

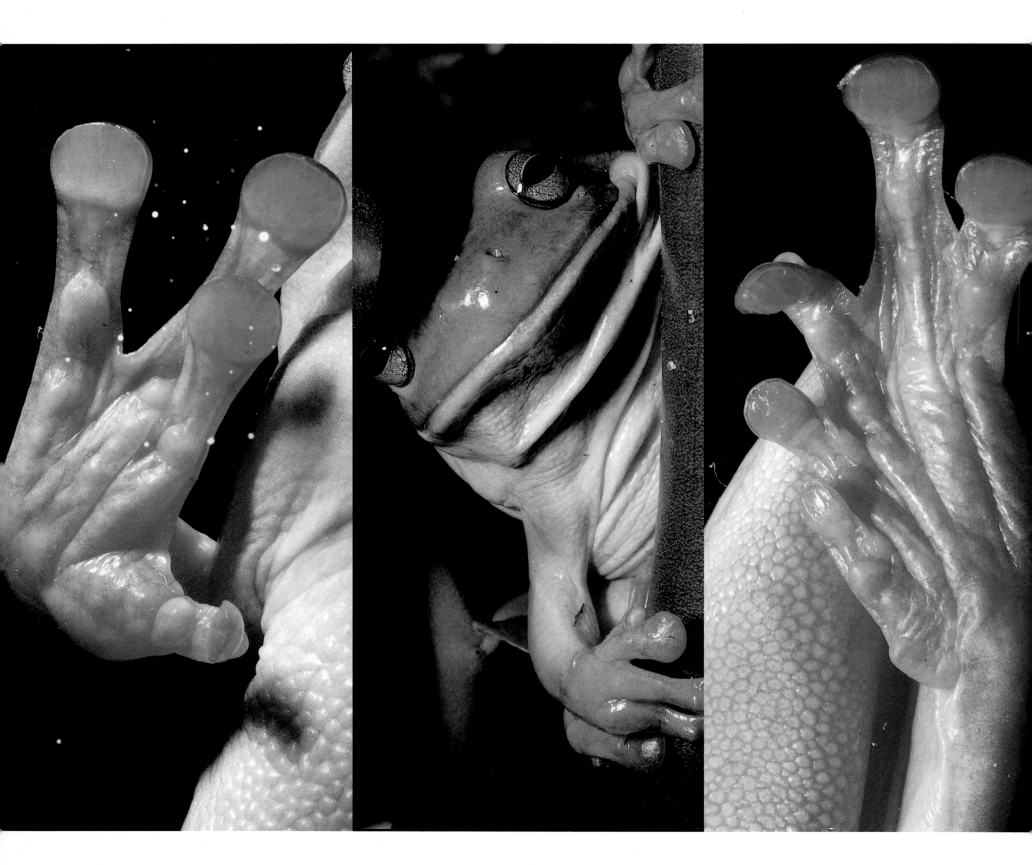

Preceding double page:

Fireworks? A colony of sea anemones? No, something much more unusual — extremely rare eucalyptus flowers (*Eucalyptus ptycocarpa*). Queensland, Australia.

Amphibian triptych: a giant tree frog (*Litoria caerulea*). Rain forest of North Queensland, Australia. The underside of its front and back legs have adhesive disks, which are essential to tree-dwellers. With these suction cups, tree frogs can attach themselves securely to leaves. Chemical pollution in lakes and rivers along the east coast of North Queensland is now endangering the local fauna. In just one year, five species of high-altitude frogs have disappeared. Their moist skins are infallible barometers for measuring the high pollution levels caused by the insecticides and fungicides sprayed over the banana and sugar cane plantations.

Like pink porcelain. *Nicolaïa sp.* Gabon. This odorless flower makes up for its lack of perfume with other charms — an array of strangely cold, smooth petals. The long outer petals are as soft as supple leather, while the inner petals make a tight bouquet of polished fingernails.

Sticky nectar flowers, which have dropped from a tree after a violent rainstorm. A cloud of parched midges flutter around them. Koulamoutou region, Gabon. Flowers often grow in a specific architectural cluster.

Fruits and flowers are low in fats and sugars, which means that gleaners eat more of them. This dispersion actually promotes greater fertilization. Right, top: Grasshopper on the fruit of a *Dillenia alata*. North Queensland, Australia. Far right, top: Shiny fruit of the *Clerodendrum floribundum*. North Queensland. Australia. Right, bottom: A nectar-rich bromeliad attracts hummingbirds. Minas Gervais, Brazil. Far right, bottom: Turmeric. Somerset Dam, Queensland, Australia.

Cauliflorous tree covered with red fruit that is highly
prized by fearsome black wasps, with painful stings.
Fruits and flowers grow directly on the trunk
of cauliflorous plants.
Swampy undergrowth, Wongua-Wongué reserve, Gabon.
A colony of nocturnal lepidopterans sleeping
during the day on a liana in a shady undergrowth.
Dry tropical forest, Tsingy de Namoroka, west Madagascar.

dusk and dawn

A most paradoxical mixture of sound and silence pervades the shady parts of the wood. The noise from the insects is so loud, that it may be heard even in a vessel anchored several hundred yards from the shore; yet within the recesses of the forest a universal silence appears to reign. To a person fond of natural history, such a day as this brings with it a deeper pleasure than he can ever hope to experience again.

Charles Darwin, *The Voyage of the Beagle*

The dark stormy sky drops lower and lower. It's the rainy season. The large helicopter flies over the thick mantle of the Gabonese forest, creating a deafening noise. Whirls of damp air carry the deepest odors of equatorial Africa to me. It's a bitter, incomparable smell of scorching laterite and the spicy scent of trees. In places, silvery blue veins of rivers disappear under dense canopies. Spirals of smoke rise from village enclaves in what looks like a parsley field, stretching as far as the eye can see. Mist covers the rounded summits of ancient mountains, shaped by thousands of years of erosion. Fallen old trees rot slowly away. Wood-eating insects, larvae, worms, and crustaceans, along with all types of mushrooms, contribute to the recycling process, feeding on the forest floor strewn with dead leaves and overripe fruit. The light offers an infinite play of chiaroscuro as the day fades into twilight. Nocturnal animals replace diurnal beasts in a cacophony of cries, screeches, wails, furtive movements, and sweet-scented or putrid breathing. I penetrate into this no-man's land on tiptoes.

A helicopter flight over the virgin forest during the rainy season. Ndangui region, Okondja, east Gabon.
"Ala," or the primary forest at the base of the Tsaratanana mountains; the highest peak is Mount Maromokotro, at 9,436 feet (2,876 meters), northeast Madagascar.
Erocoïde shrubs grow on the summits. The region is extremely hard to reach: it takes one week to hike to the top. This mountain jungle arbors rare orchids, various species of palm trees, tree ferns, and forests of endemic bamboo.
Nocturnal white tree frog (*Heterixalus madagascariensis*). Racophoridae. Pangalanes swamp, east coast of Madagascar.

Early morning. I'm walking through the damp forest after a torrential rainfall during the night. It's monsoon season. I look up, hearing sharp screeches; a pair of weaver birds are building a net-shaped curving nest. These "architect-birds" weave their family home with elegance and precision. Flat on my stomach on a bed of sodden moss, I frame a strange mushroom, covered with a white lacy veil. A relative of the European phallacae, this tropical variant attracts clouds of flies, with the musk-like, cadaverous odor of its gelatin. What a strange symbol, just a few feet from the couple of weaver "love-birds!" Phallacae with a lace frill. (*Dictyophora multicolor*). Pangalanes, Madagascar.

It's night and the moon is rising as I explore the swamp. Suddenly, an extraordinary perfume fills the air, sweeping aside my fear. I discover small green stars at the base of a tree. They have a divine fragrance — a blend of syringa, jasmine, rose, and narcissus.
Right, top: furry aquatic lilies. North Queensland, Australia.
Far right, top: Geaster (*Geaster fimbriatus*). Forest in northeast Madagascar.
Bottom, right: Primitive, sticky flower (*Eupomortia bennettii*). Mission Beach rain forest, North Queensland, Australia.
Bottom, far right: Nebulous lepiota. Jungle near Cardwell, North Queensland, Australia.

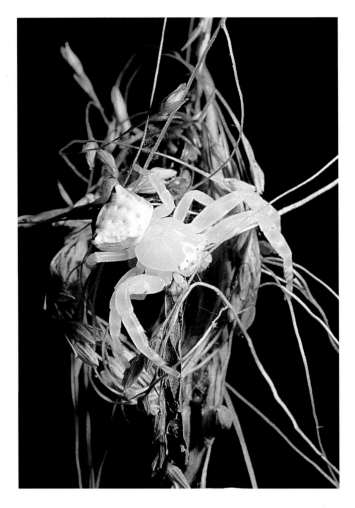

Crab-spider lying in ambush in its unusual trap, a sheaf of grass coated with a sticky thread. It's lethal to passing insects, as the trap is set up in the open air. The wind diverts the unfortunate butterflies, midges, and dragonflies onto the sticky threads.
Lakefield N.P., Australia.

A spiky-backed chameleon (*Chamaeleo pardalis*) on giant orchids (*Angraecum eburneum*). Madagascar has some thirty Chameleonidae of the *Chamaeleo* genus. Despite international laws protecting endangered species, orchids, and chameleons are sold at great profit; this traffic thrives on illegal markets.

Previous double page:
Sunrise in the Malagasy forest. Tamatave region, Madagascar. The surface area of world's forests now measures 8.9 million acres (3.5 million hectares), but each year thousands of acres of tropical forest go up in smoke.

Caryocar brazilensis. Relic forests of Minas Gerais, Brazil. The fragrance is a subtle blend of daffodil, freesia, and fresh coriander, with a touch of vanilla. Scents are stronger at night, and sometimes lead the way to rare flowers.

Tree frog (*Litoria fallox*) on stalks of very rare black orchids (*Cymbidium canalieulatum*). Caulderslake, Lakefield, N.P., Australia.
A camp in an idyllic spot where these black orchids — unique in the world — were growing. One week later, the site would be ravaged by flames.

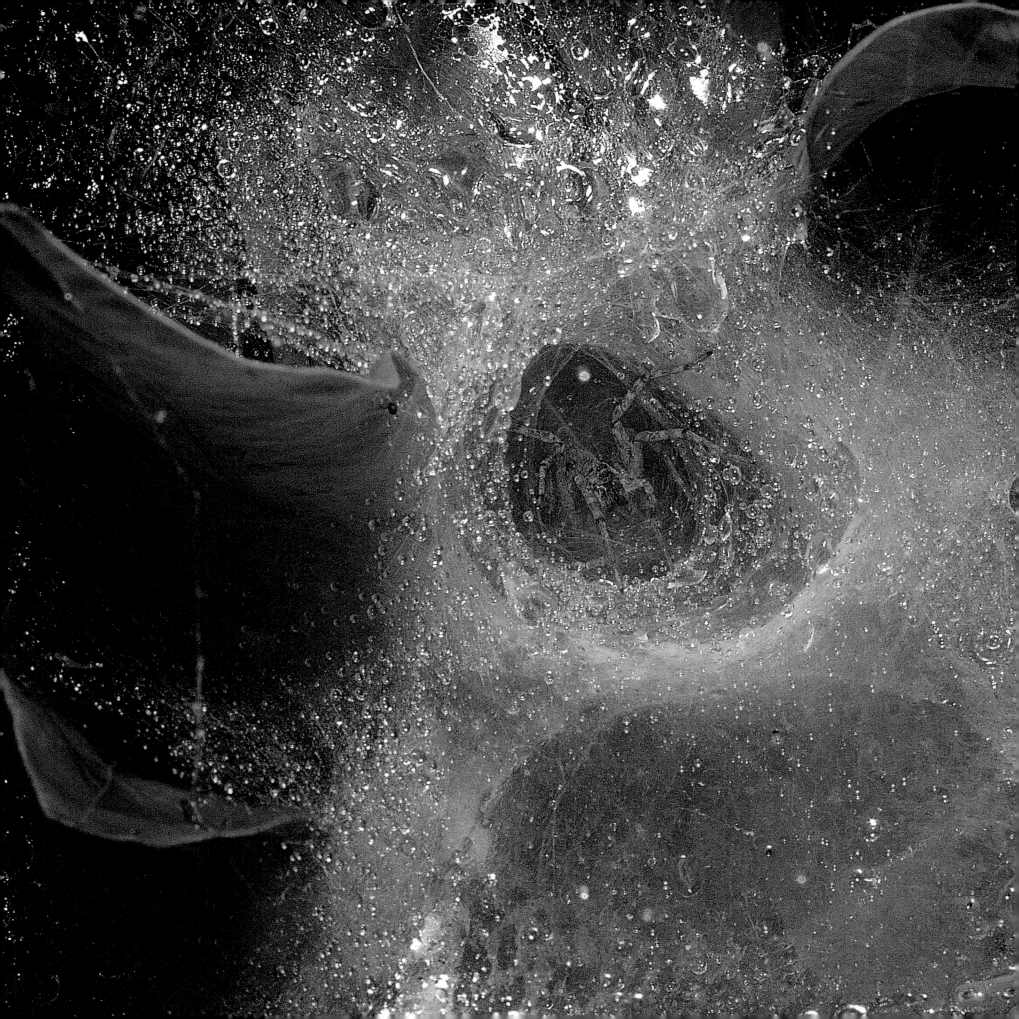

This oblong spider's web, stretching several meters at the base of some shrubs, glitters with raindrops. In the center are hidden tunnels leading to the spider's lair. This invisible web traps insects and small lizards in its mortal weave. Spiders spin their webs with a long, sticky, and extremely strong adhesive thread secreted from their abdomens. The structure of the weave varies with each species. Suitors announce their arrival by tapping on the web in a particular way, distinct from that of prey. It's a cannibalistic love affair, however, unless the male manages to tie up his partner with her own silk thread. Forêt des Abeilles. Gabon.

Dewdrops dot dead leaves on the forest floor. Australia. Plants "breathe" and "perspire" through their pores (stomatas).

A 98-foot (30-meter) waterfall on the Namorona, in Betsileo, south of Fianarantsoa, Madagascar. The heat is oppressive; the air saturated with humidity. It's monsoon season, when torrential rains cut ravines through the red clay ground, and overflow rivers and torrents. The rutted old track is lined with trucks and off-road vehicles stuck in the mud up to their doors. Orchids, lemurs, multicolored butterflies, tenrecs (mini-hedgehogs) and fosas (extremely rare wild felines) roam in the nearby forests. They are fortunate to still have these refuges: deforestation has caused major damage to the large island of Madagascar.

Life could have been created right here, in this far corner of our planet. For millions of years, the earth was bombarded by meteorite showers. Traces of them remain to this day in the form of craters filled with deep lakes or dense jungles. Certain American exobiologists, after analyzing amino acids found in meteorite fragments, have deduced that life on earth came from outer space.

Stalks of giant orchids (*Angraecum eburneum*).
Hygrophile forest on the east coast, Pangalanes,
Madagascar. Madagascar is home to more than
12,000 species of plants, 85 percent of which are
endemic.

Comet (*Angraecum sesquipedale*). This is the queen of
Malagasy orchids (780 species). Measuring 4 inches
(10 cm) across, it has a 14-inch (35-cm) style. It can
be pollinated by only a single moth (*Xanthopan
morgani*), drawn to its heady scent, which resembles
tuberose. The moth's 12-inch (30-cm) proboscis can
drink the nectar buried deep within. In exchange, the
insect spreads the orchid's pollen.

Following double page: **Twilight** over the Indonesian
jungle. Java, Indonesia.

bright nights

East coast of North Queensland. 5:30 in the evening. Like immense black lips, clouds part to reveal a mouth of fire. The night wind blows away this celestial fresco. I emerge from the belly of the swampy jungle. I feel something observing me. To the left, an immense black eye shining in the half-light watches me. The owl remains perched a few seconds then flies off without a sound. We take the same direction. I'm heading northward.

6:50 P.M. The jungle grows increasingly louder. Invisible in the darkness, creatures arrayed in feathers, fur, scales, powder or mucus take over from the diurnal species. I splash through the muck of a stream hidden by rampant ferns. Is this an optical illusion? A human-shaped tree scares me to death. My anxiety grows. Incandescent eyes shine in a puddle of water. A cane-toad contorts its body grotesquely as it swallows a butterfly. An iridescent python slithers lazily along a tree trunk. My head lamp stops working. Stars reflecting in a puddle keep me from falling into a swamp. Danger increases tenfold at night: there are no landmarks, it's impossible to judge distances, poisonous snakes look like liana or roots. I'm frightened of something I can't see, yet feel to be close by. Reprieve? Survival?

*I recall the mysterious impenetrable solitude
of the jungle, a solitude alive, if one is
equipped with knowledge, with a ceaseless
warfare of winged and crawling hosts.*

William McFee, *The Market*

Preceding double page: **Owl** (*Ninox connivens*),
16 inches (40 cm) long. Its cry? Woo-hoo! Woo-boo!
Who calls in this deep blue night? This strigiforme has
a squat body, with a large head and powerful talons.
Jungle between Bingil Bay and Mission Beach, North
Queensland, Australia.
Night in the virgin forest. Great lakes region of
Lambaréné, Gabon.
A passion flower (*Passiflora sp*) from the Tableland
region of North Queensland.
A dragonfly asleep in a clearing at sundown. Its
wings are iridescent as they reflect the setting sun.
North Queensland, Australia.

Echidna (*Tachyglossus aculeatus*). This primitive
oviparous mammal is toothless and feeds on termites.
Its coat of long quills, like a porcupine's, and two
venomous spurs on its rear legs offer effective
protection from predators (birds of prey and dingoes).
Steep forest, Dunk Island, Australia.
Pink and black nocturnal tree frog (*Phrynomerus
bifasciatus*). Central Africa.

Pangolin (*Manis javanica*). This tree anteater, protected by a thick armor of ossified scales, feeds on termites and ants. Javanese jungle, Indonesia.

I hear the muffled sound of bats flying out of their caves. I was fast asleep in my hammock, protected from undesirable creatures (scorpions and spiders) when something smacked into my mosquito netting. A frightened bat is limping along the ground. Perhaps its radar, which can identify a target at a frequency of 100 ultrasonic waves per second, wasn't working. Most likely, it was fooled by the fine khaki-colored netting. It then climbed awkwardly onto a trunk before taking off again. Virgin forest, Mitzing, Gabon.

Full moon and midnight blue sky. The rare frogmouth (*Podargus ocellatus*) feeds on reptiles, frogs, rodents, and animal carcasses. It can detect any prey within a radius of 650 feet (200 meters), thanks to the light-colored feathers around its eye that act as a funnel, amplifying the light. Cape York Peninsula, North Queensland, Australia.

Owls on the prowl screech at each other intermittently; insects vibrate their elytra, squeak their hind legs. I turn on my pocket-recorder to capture the sounds of these palavers. A pinkish moon rises over the forest edge. Walls of liana form twisted braids of garlands and shrouds around trees. I keep watch from the hammock waiting for total darkness. The hell with the mosquito net! A nocturnal bird with blood-red eyes and striped beige plumage soars over my head. One of its soft feathers drifts down onto my chest. It has a strange scent of dust and wheat.

Owl (*Otus rufescens*). Dry tropical forest, Berenty Reserve, south Madagascar.

At night, owls hear via a sonar-like system called echolocation.

The stars are shining. A moth tickles my neck, sucking on drips of sweat. A small shape moves along the path. It's a potto — an extremely rare nocturnal lemur (*Arctocebus calabarensis*) that lives in the thick forest. During the day, it sleeps in a hollow tree trunk or in branches. In case of danger, it secretes a viscous substance from its anus that reeks of musk and rotten shrimp. Forêt des Abeilles, Gabon.

A nocturnal gecko (*Gehyra sp.*), 5 inches (12 cm) long, shedding its skin, discovered asleep under an old stump after laying its eggs — two calcified eggs approximately 1/2 inch (1 cm) long. It squeals when I capture it. The scaly skin feels like velvet. Like certain other lizards, geckos can release their tails (a characteristic known as autotomy) to escape an enemy. It grows back in a few months. Top End of Cape York, North Queensland, Australia.
Horned frog (*Megophris montana*). Indonesia. Magnificent and sticky, this frog stakes out a hideout in a tunnel of dead leaves and waits for earthworms.

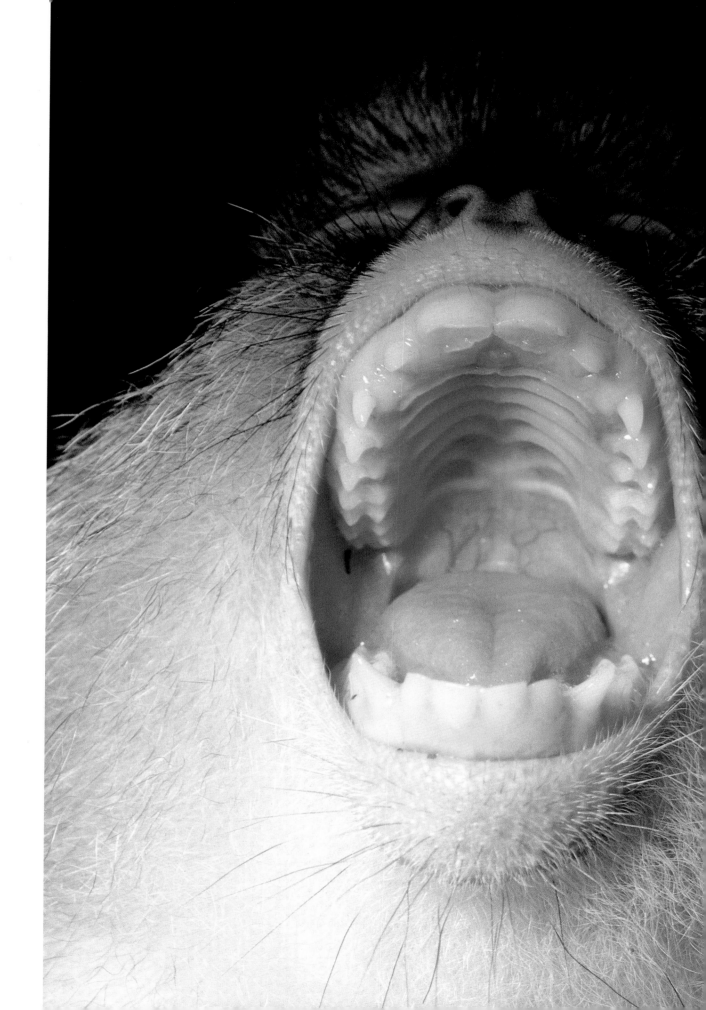

Aggressive as a bad-tempered little runt, this young long-snouted crocodile (*Crocodylus cataphractus*) wails in despair when I capture it. Trapped by the neck, it tries to bite me. Its small teeth are as sharp as razors and can inflict infectious wounds. Once they reach adulthood, these amphibian reptiles can be up to 11 1/2 feet (3.5 meters) long. It swims using webbed feet and caudal propulsion. When underwater, it can block ears, nostrils, and throat, while its eyes are protected by a third, colorless lid, a nictitating membrane. Completely sealed off, it lies in wait, mouth open to swallow fish, frogs, and toads as they swim by. Kango Forest, Gabon.

Cercopithecus (*Cercopythecus mona*) howling in its "dormitory." Gabon. Never smile or show your teeth to a monkey: it considers this to be threatening, and it could bite.

deadly forest

Salt Creek, Cape York Peninsula, Australia.

The amber sky is covered with thousands of blue feathers. The clouds form an immense condor, its wings spread over the drowsy bush. 5:15 P.M. It's starting to get cold. I have horrible, purulent blisters on my hands and forearms. It's a foul night! Marshflies, mosquitoes, and midges are making my life miserable. These loathsome flying creatures carry dangerous fevers and parasites. I set up camp overlooking the Salt River, a region of mangroves and gallery-forest. The river is higher than usual. Water temperature: 72° F (22° C). Dependent on the incoming tide, the enormous salt-water crocodiles — from 13 to 16 1/2 feet (4 to 5 meters) long — frolic here at night. I can spot their incandescent eyes in the beam of my flashlight. A long silvery wake breaks the black surface of the river. Splashing water and snapping jaws betray the presence of these man-eaters. A massive greenish head, covered with slimy algae, emerges from the water. I watch it carefully from my hiding place behind some shrubs. Suddenly, a hairy creature skims over my fingers. I scream! The hideous large and deadly wolf spider flees as fast as it can.

Vigilance is the path to immortality;
nonchalance, the way to death.

Dhammapada, The Sayings of Buddha

Riverbed and *Tristania sp.* These giant trees grow on the outer edge of the mangrove belt. Hinchinbrook Island, Australia.

A mangrove (*Rhyzophora*) swamp. Malibé, Gabon. This labyrinth of impenetrable roots is infested with mosquitoes; it is a hell of stinking, briny mud. Getting through it requires unbelievable gymnastics: I climb over the arched roots of the mangrove to keep from sinking. A compass is essential, and you have to watch out for the incoming tide.

Rhyzophora **mangrove.** Indonesia. These endangered amphibious forests serve as ecological niches for mollusks, crustaceans, fish, and crocodiles. Depending on the tide, the intertwined

roots are flooded, then left high and dry. They acquire oxygen through lenticels that close during high tide.

Nile crocodile (*Crocodylus niloticus*). 19 1/2 feet (6 meters) maximum. Ogooué, Gabon. Giant crocodiles sometimes attack fishermen in African rivers or the mangrove channels in Australia, flipping over boats with a tail lash, then devouring the occupants.

Strangling fig tree (*Ficus sp.*). Lake Eacham, North Queensland, Australia. After years spent together, this parasite has finally overcome its host. Anchored in the ground by lianiforme roots, this fig tree is suffocating the tree that has been supporting it.

Johnston crocodile (*Crocodylus johnstonii*). Rare.
11 1/2 feet (3.5 meters). Cape York Peninsula. North
Queensland, Australia.
Teeth of the salt-water crocodile (*Crocodylus porosus*).
North Queensland. Adults can be 23 feet (7 meters)
long. These "salites" will attack humans. Their powerful
jaws can inflict fearsome wounds, which can become
gangrenous. Crocodiles grow new teeth throughout their
lives. Among the *Crocodylus,* the fourth tooth on the
lower jaw fits into a notch in the upper jaw, and
the fifth tooth of the upper jaw is the longest of all.

An 11-1/2 foot (3.5-meter) black-and-white cobra (*Naja melanoleuca*). Ivory Coast. In the bush, every second can bring tragedy. Death, camouflaged in the recesses of the shadows, strikes quickly. This cobra has adopted an intimidating stance, with its hood spread. At rest, a cobra looks just like any other snake. Thousands of people die every year, poisoned by the neurotoxic venom of the cobra.

Frilled-neck lizard (*Chlamydosaurus kingii*). These conical teeth inflict cruel wounds. North Queensland, Australia.

Wagler's pit viper (*Trimeresurus waglerii*). Ujun Kulong National Park, Java, Indonesia. The multicolored finery of this crotalidae translates into certain death for any absent-minded bird. This highly poisonous tree snake injects a hemotoxic and neurotoxic venim with its retractable fangs and feeds on rodents, birds, and lizards. A crotadilae or "pit viper" has a heat-sensitive pit between its eye and nostril, which detects warm-blooded prey.

Young crocodiles (*Crocodylus johnstonii*). Rare.
Musgrave region. Cape York Peninsula, Australia.
Frogmouth (*Podargus papuaguinea*). Wing span:
4 feet (1.2 meters). Its large hard beak is useful for
killing prey: reptiles, rodents, and amphibians.
I encountered this rare bird drowned in a pond.
The bird, blanketed with scavenger ants, died from
intestinal paristitosis — a sad end for this red-eyed
nocturnal phantom. Cape York Peninsula, Australia.

Spiked liana (*Calamus sp.*) Hinchinbrook Island, Australia.

Leaves rustling in the hot wind. Long, high-pitched whistles end sharply. An olive-green whip bird stops to drink at the river where I'm bathing, in a pool covered with soft algae. It's too bad this tropical Eden is swarming with all kinds of parasites, carriers of illnesses that strike thousands of people throughout the world every year: malaria, dengue fever, bilharziosis, yellow fever, and filariosis, to name a few. Gooey, empty leeches on the forest floor move like caterpillars. Parched for warm blood, they head my way. Laminghton Range rain forest, Queensland, Australia.

A deadly poisonous bird snake (*Thelothornis kirtlandii*) on a raffia palm, Mondah forest, Gabon. The *Thelothornis* has a fast-acting neurotoxic venom; it lures prey – small birds – by wriggling its bright red tongue like a small earthworm. This is the only tree snake that uses such a strategy. In the jungle, poison is a common weapon among both animals and plants: serpents, frogs and toads, insects, fruit, seeds, leaves, flowers with noxious scents, and liana with strychnine or cyanide. Humans, at the end of the ecological chain, are unrivaled in their use of poisons to heal or destroy their own kind. Traditional healers know that for many poisonous plants, its antidote often grows nearby.

Tree snake (*Boiga dendrophylla*) ready to attack. Its forked tongue is also an olfactory organ. Java Jungle, Indonesia.

Nature's drama: creatures devour each other against spectacular backdrops.

Left, top: A battle between queen green ants (*Oecophylla smaragdina*). Queensland, Australia. These weaver ants construct their nests by using their mandibles to join together leaves with a silk thread secreted by the larvae. Queens live about twenty years (while workers live only two to three years) and are highly prized by aborigines, who love this protein-rich food.

Left, bottom: Striped snake swallowing a frog. Indonesia.

Carnivorous pitcher plants (*Nepenthes madagascariensis*). Peat bogs of Pangalanes, Madagascar. The deep pitchers contain a deadly enzymatic liquid that digests the plant's prey (insects, fledglings, lizards). Their nectary glands emit a heady musk-like scent that attracts clouds of insects. When it rains, a red operculum closes over the top of the pitcher. Only one species of frog can enter this receptacle to steal a few butterflies with impunity: its adhesive disks help it to climb back up the deadly smooth walls of the flower.

Inside story. My attention is caught by the green flowers of the *Eucalyptus viridiflora* that have fallen to the ground. Suddenly I discover an incredible caterpillar, bristling with quills like a porcupine. Its armor of venomous stingers, arrayed like branches or darts, acts as a defense against birds or the merely curious (nausea and convulsions guaranteed). But the caterpillar is writhing strangely: an ant is trying to rip it open in a pint-sized battle of David and Goliath. Lakefield, Cape York Peninsula, North Queensland, Australia.

Common chameleon (*Chamaeleo chamaeleone*) devouring a grasshopper. Wongua-Wongué Reserve, Gabon.

Carisco mangrove bay, **Gabon.** A swampy zone of rhizophores and raffias. It's 97° F (36° C) in the shade at the edge of the forest, and 81° F (27° C) under cover of the forest.

A colobus monkey killed by hunters. Bitam region, on the border between Gabon and Equatorial Guinea. The profitable traffic of "bush meat" is growing at an alarming rate, seriously endangering the equilibrium of the forests. Steel wire snares are multiplying on paths worn down by poachers and native hunters. It's a nightmare for wild animals; some suffer atrociously, then rot where they died. Other terrifying traps, such as large holes concealed by branches, maim and kill elephants, buffalo, and warthogs.

hide-and-seek

Every manifestation of nature is subject to the law of causality.

Fo-Sho-Hing-Tsan-King

Leaning against a large tree trunk, I watch the activities of diurnal and nocturnal animals. In my khaki fatigues, waterproof poncho that fits over my backpack, high rubber boots, cap with a wide visor, and mosquito net over my face, I blend in with the decor. I watch the events of the untamed world, its games of cruel or gentle seductive hide-and-seek as a delighted and sometimes anxious spectator. Hunting? Mating? There are all kinds of animal activities in coded language in this plant cauldron that swarms constantly with insects and frogs on the ground, in the air, under the water: billions of visual, acoustic, olfactory, or chemical signals. Green animals hide in the plants; brown ones on the forest floor and against tree trunks and branches; gray or beige creatures on beds of algae or moss, in silt or muddied waters. To escape predators, old or wounded animals use ruse and camouflage. In the bush, I sleep with one eye and ear open, given that there is always something, somewhere, which threatens. I often extract myself from my bivouacs shivering from cold, fear, and dread.

Previous page and left:
Green day gecko (*Phelsuma madagascariensis*) hidden behind a *Pandanus* palm tree. Pangalanes, Madagascar. This small lizard is an exception among the Gekkonidae, which are usually nocturnal. It feeds on insects, sleeping at night, awake during the day. Its excellent visual acuity is perfectly adapted to the rapid movement of its prey. Gekkonidae, like snakes, are characterized by their large eyes with elliptical pupils, covered with colorless membranes. Other distinguishing features: a velvety or grainy skin formed of scales arranged side by side and five-toed feet that adhere securely thanks to thousands of microscopic hooks.
The time of two gekkos: one, pointing straight up, indicating noon; the other at 2 o'clock. Despite its camouflage, it is betrayed by a ray of sunshine.

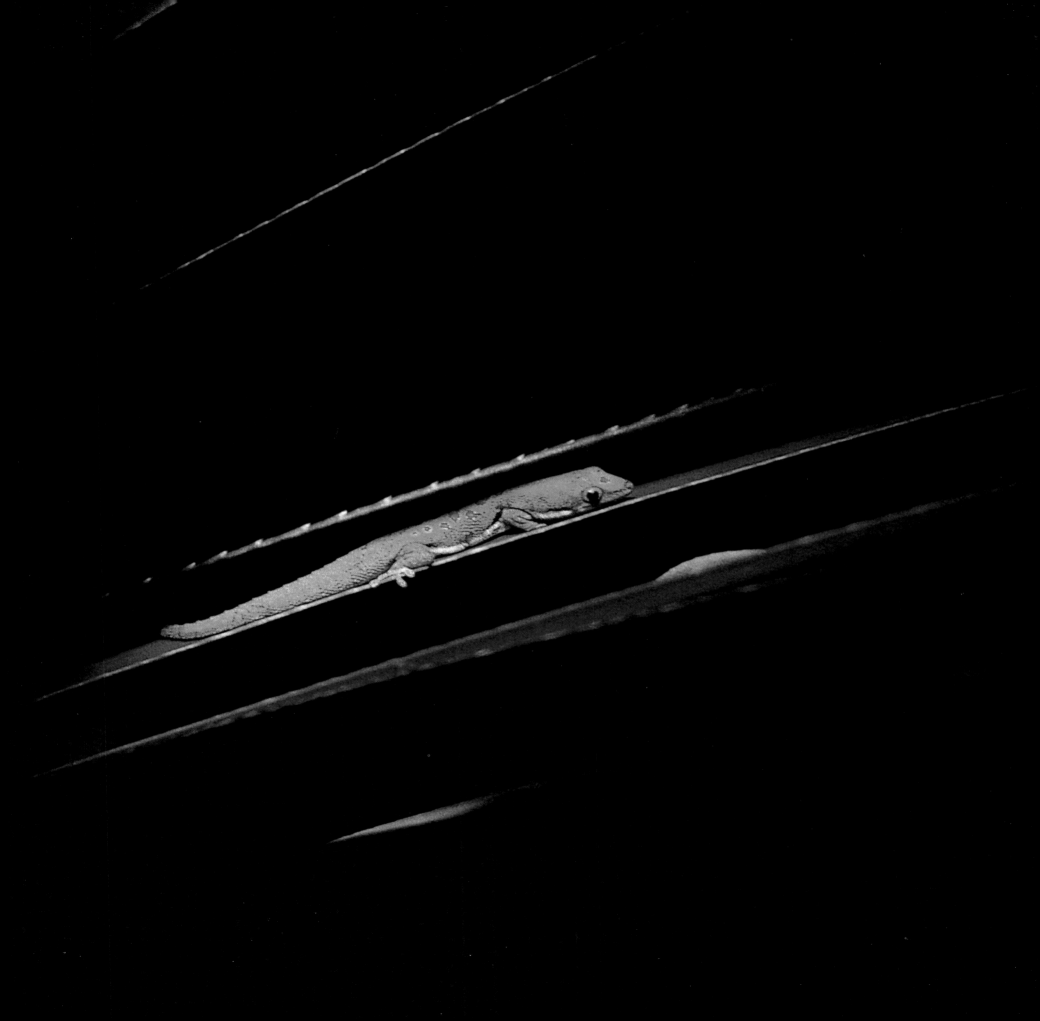

The name chameleon comes from the Greek word *khamaileôn,* or "dwarf lion." This small tree saurien is found in the forests of Africa and Asia. Left, top: a young Gabonese chameleon (*Chamaeleo chamaeleone*) lies in wait for insects. His circular eyelids, retracted as far as they will go, conceal a tiny hole, its eye. To capture prey, it thrusts out its tongue, which is covered with a sticky mass, and is as long as or even longer than its own body.

Left, bottom: Chameleon (*Chamaeleo dilepis*) in camouflage. This one is angry: its skin has turned dark green and is covered with yellow spots. At night, skin color often becomes lighter. During the day, when the sun is too hot, the chameleon adopts bright colors that can reflect the sun's rays. When it is cold, on the other hand, skin turns a darker color to better absorb the heat. An ousted rival turns a dull grayish color, while the victor sports the brightest possible colors.

Right: **Green tree snake** waits in ambush (*Dryophis nasuta*). Java Jungle, Indonesia.

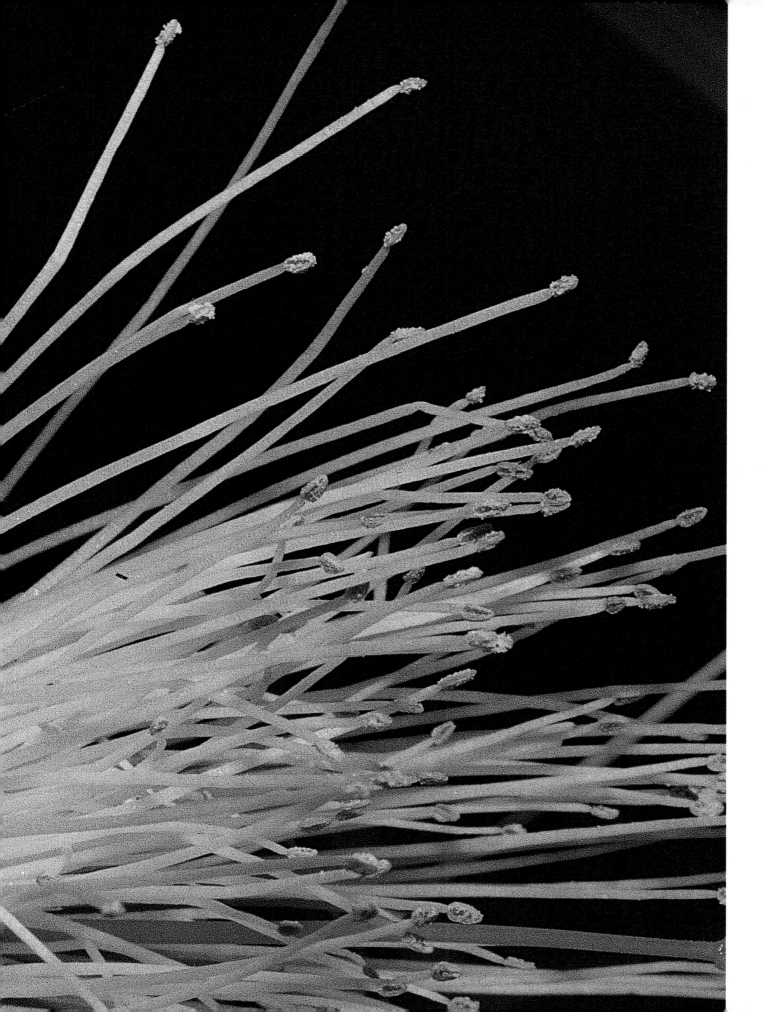

A Mantoidae lies in wait on flowers of a *Planchonia careyia*. During a stormy night, not far from Daly River (North Territory, Australia), my head lamp shines on a miniature black beetle gorging itself on nectar. He disappears when he catches sight of me. I move closer toward the magnificent white flowers and discover this praying mantis waiting in ambush. It must have been anticipating a meal of the greedy insect, whose life I unknowingly saved. Meanwhile, above this miniature theater, the sky bombards the forest with thunder and lightning, before the deluge of the monsoon strikes.

Nature is prolific in terms of disguises, and has created some of the strangest imaginable forms. Left, top: A wisp of straw taking a stroll? No, it's a 2-inch (6-cm) stick insect. In case of danger, it freezes and blends in with the twigs. Mondah Forest, Gabon. Left, bottom: Dumeril monitor lizard (*Varanus dumerilii*). Indonesia. Like serpents, monitor lizards often stick out their long, tubular forked tongues to "smell" for the trace of rodents and frogs. Each tip of the tongue transmits the scented particles of its prey to the "Jacobsen's organ," an olfactory radar in the roof of the mouth. When chasing prey in water, it swims like a crocodile, using caudal propulsion, and can stay underwater more than one hour.

Chameleons can transform into perfect copies of the shapes and colors of the substratum, becoming virtually invisible. Their large protruding eyes rotate independently, watching for insects or a rapacious predator. Madagascar.

A nighttime encounter, just after a rainfall, at the base of a moss-covered tree. This prehistoric spiny cricket (*Eugaster sp.*) jerks forward like a robot. Soft, silky, and cooperative, it lets me take its portrait in a few seconds. Back and legs sting my fingers when I touch. With regret, I let this rare creature go. Monts de Cristal Forest, Gabon.

A rustling in the leaves: a skink (*Lampropholis challengerii*) scurries between two dead leaves. Bingil Bay, North Queensland, Australia.

This 6-inch (12-cm) oviparous lizard belongs to the family Scincidae. They have smooth overlapping scales making it easier for them to crawl over a forest floor strewn with obstacles.

A platypus or duckbill (*Ornithorynchus anatus*). Atherton, Tableland, Australia. This aquatic duckbilled oviparous mammal feeds on fish and crustaceans. It has two fearsome venomous spurs on its back legs, which can kill a rabbit in minutes.
Tree ferns, originally from New Guinea: before continental drift, Australia and New Guinea were connected. The first 33-foot (10-meter) ferns appeared on earth during the Carboniferous era, some 350 million years ago. A pair of royal parrots with scarlet plumage squabble in this protected Eden. Lake Eacham, North Queensland, Australia.

The temperature is dropping. Pied crows fly across the darkened sky. A sparrow breaks free from the undergrowth. A small beige lemur with wide orange eyes sits in the fork of a large tree with acid green leaves. The *Lepilemur* is just leaving its nest, a hole in a large tree trunk. It loves plants, insects, and small mollusks, but can, if food is lacking elsewhere, eat its own excrement. Berenty Reserve, south Madagascar.

A shiny wake cuts through the surface of the water. A mangrove snake (*Boiga dendrophylla*), swimming downstream in the river swollen after a rainfall. Ujun-Kulong, Java, Indonesia.

The camouflaged author, amazed by all these intimate manifestations of nature. I have no gun or radio; every day, I change my itinerary, improvising new camps. In general, I radiate in a star formation around the same spot, over a distance of 6 to 18 miles (10 to 30 km).

Undergrowth. Swarms of frightened black and white butterflies, 2 inches (6 cm) across, flutter everywhere. The air in this small space hums with their quivering wings. No luck for the photo — they're moving too much. A kookaburra with mottled beige wings snickers. I can see it from the back. Between two arpeggios, it raises its tail to reveal a pinkish rump. A branch falls to the ground. The sky is an intense blue. Hygrophile forest. El Arish, North Queensland, Australia.

eyes
of the jungle

Look deep within and you will see music.
The heart of nature is filled with music.
You just have to reach it.

Thomas Carlyle

Two golden orbs emerge from the foliage to my right. A snake! I'm delighted! This one, with a long green nose and gray-blue tongue, is as thin as wire; it sways imperceptibly to keep a better eye on everything moving in the forest and to maintain its balance. In the background, I hear the constant murmuring of a river lined with sprawling trees. The night will soon fall. I am dripping in sweat. My jacket is splattered with mud, stuck through with twigs, and covered with bits of gray spider webs I broke through on the path, and spots of blood from the dozens of marshflies and mosquitoes I squashed. The heat is sweltering. The Indonesian jungle is closing in. Macaques howl in the distance. Two violet dragonflies sleep on a fern. Tree frogs open their green eyelids, revealing red eyes. Each of these animals, hidden in the various layers of the forest, has a magical expression. I'm always frightened when I explore the jungle on my own, both during the day and at night. Frightened of these thousands of invisible eyes that I can't identify — spying, assessing, and even innocent eyes. I'm frightened of my own shadow in front of or behind me, depending on the direction of the path and the lunar light. Frightened of whatever danger may lie a few steps ahead or behind.

Page 181: **Vine snake** (*Dryophis nasuta*) lit from the back. Java Jungle, Indonesia. This magical encounter in a bamboo forest led to an impromptu capture. The snake curled up as I stroked it; we both enjoyed the contact. It was extremely velvety and fine to the touch, as if it had just sloughed its skin.

Vine snake (*Dryophis nasuta*) in a posture of observation. Serpents, or ophidians, are deaf, but they have extremely keen senses of sight and smell to help them detect their prey. Somewhere near the hungry snake may be its quarry, a frog well-hidden in the leaves, or a sharp-eyed deadly bird of prey. In accordance with the implacable law of the food chain, the predator will ultimately experience the same fate as its victim.

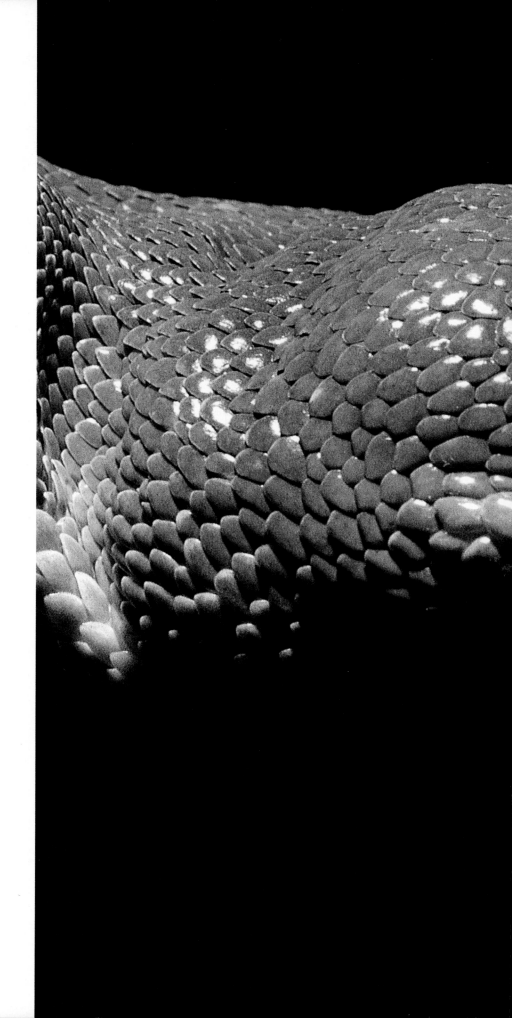

Green tree viper (*Atheris chlorechis*). The elliptical pupil of this nocturnal species retracts depending on the intensity of the light. It is a solenoglyph: it has two 1-inch (2-cm) venomous fangs, which retract like a cat's claws. The hemotoxic venom causes death by blood coagulation. Tamed, this snake shared my camp for several weeks. Its overlapping scales were rough to the touch. Taï Forest, Ivory Coast.

Blue python (*Chondropython viridis*). Rare. The serpent's eyes are protected by a transparent lid or "eyeglass." The lack of a movable pupil is what gives the impression that snakes have a fixed stare – hence the myth of hypnotic serpents. In fact, its prey is paralyzed more by fear than by the snake's eyes.

Eyes receive electromagnetic vibrations in waves ranging from 0.75 to 0.45 microns; these are analyzed by the brain's occipital lobe and transformed into colors and images.

Far left, top: The orange eyes of a giant tree frog (*Litoria infrafrenata*). North Queensland, Australia. Like a fish-eye lens, its large protruding eyes have a wide field of vision and can magnify the ambient light. Its croaking sound resembles something like a guttural bark or the sound of a bag of nuts being shaken.

Left, top: Eye of a 16-foot (4.8-meter) python (*Liasis amethystinus*). Rare. Rain forest, north of Cardwell, Australia.

Far left, bottom: Snake eye (*Dryophis nasuta*). Java Jungle, Indonesia.

Left, bottom: The eye of this opisthoglyph (a snake with rear venomous fangs) is different from those of other snakes: the pupil is horizontal, rather than round, elliptical, or vertical.

Blue-eyed dragon (*Gonocephalus leiogaster*). Rare. Borneo, Indonesia.

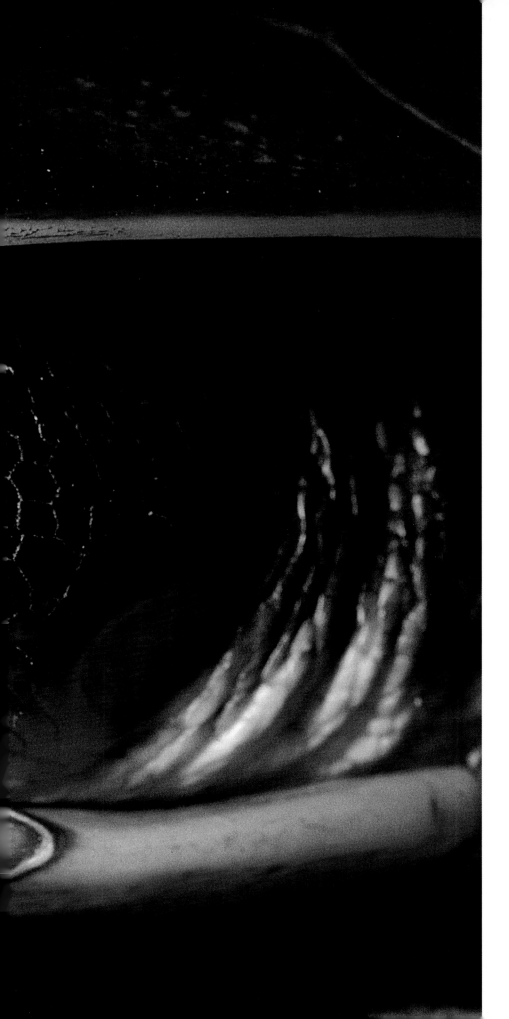

One morning, preoccupied with photographing a multicolored caterpillar, I suddenly heard a noise like a stampede. This long-necked large aquatic tortoise was about to escape right out from under me into the swamp. The chase was on; the capture, chaotic. Covered with mud, we soon came to an understanding: in exchange for photographs, I used my tweezers to remove a ring of voracious leeches attached between its hind legs. The *Chelodina rugosa* then fled. Cape York Peninsula, Australia.

Eye of a dwarf crocodile (*Osteolaemus tetraspis*). Crocodiles can see as well at night as during the day. The tapetum membrane over their eyes makes it easier to hunt at night: they turn red under the beam of my lamp. Lake Elywawanyé, Wongua-Wongué, Gabon.

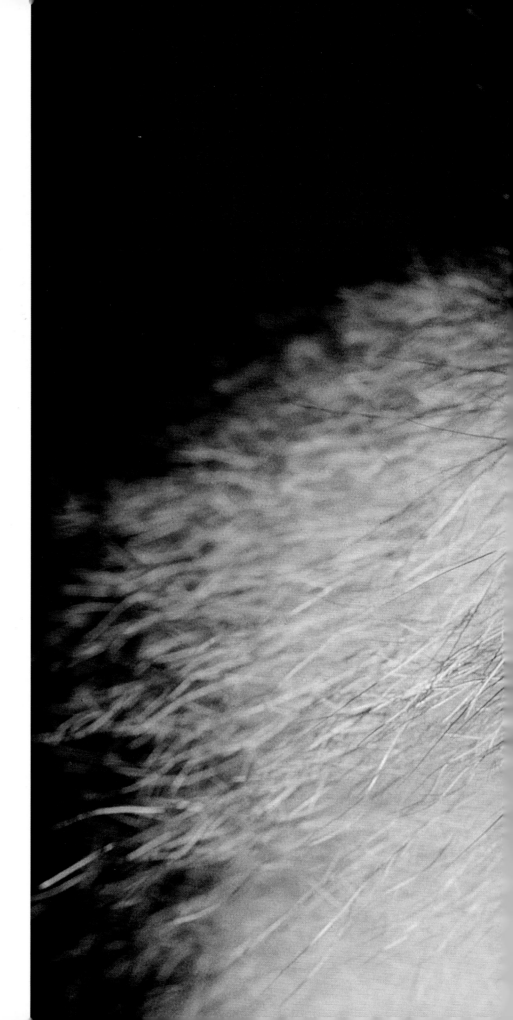

An **unexpected encounter** between two primates, one
a forest-dweller, the other, civilized. Lying in wait in my
hammock, I watch this furry creature move closer,
staring at me with its large lemon-yellow eyes. I whistle
to catch its attention. It drops from branch to branch and
is emboldened enough to fiddle with the strings of the
hammock. It seems intrigued by this unusual material.
With a few giant leaps, he disappears into the forest
canopy. Verreaux propithecus (*Propithecus verreauxi*).
Dry tropical forest, Berenty Reserve, south Madagascar.
Cercopithecus (*Cercopithecus mona*). Gabon. If you get
lost in the jungle, you can survive by following the
monkeys: everything they eat is also edible for humans.
But the taste might be far from appetizing.

yesterday and tomorrow

The chess-board is the world; the pieces are the phenomena of the universe; the rules of the game are what we call the laws of Nature. The player on the other side is hidden from us. We know that his play is always fair, and patient. But we also know, to our cost, that he never overlooks a mistake, or makes the smallest allowance for ignorance.

Thomas Henry Huxley, *A Liberal Education*

A pink flash streaks over the sleeping earth. I don't know what gates of Hell I have just opened, but I follow the call of its mystery! I turn off my head lamp. The only light in this darkness is the red lamp of my pocket recorder. At this hour, the bush has a strong scent: a sweet-and-sour odor of peat and closed flowers. The swamp reflects a moon eroded by a leprous blackness: algae and rushes crush and pierce the image, while the storm clouds swallow it up altogether. This is the magic of a wide-awake world. Adventure is right at my heels. It is my reason for living, despite the anguish, the blues, the physical exhaustion, the wounds, and the illnesses. Capturing the beauty of nature is also a way of fighting to preserve it, to raise awareness. Yesterday and tomorrow: to cross borders and time zones to discover, in total freedom, nature's creatures and their secret territories. Behind me I hear the gentle noise of a spring. Animals are moving through the forest. Thunder and lightning—louder and louder! Crickets and grasshoppers pack up and move before the deluge strikes. I pull on my waterproof poncho and plunge into this violent, superb, tropical night. A night when the world could end. Monsoon forest, somewhere 90 miles (150 km) southwest of Darwin, North Territory, Australia.

ACKNOWLEDGMENTS

AUSTRALIA: Bruce Arthur, Sandy Cloud. Richie and Debbie Carrigan. David Cooper. Don Dunstan. Peter Gould. Frieda Jorrissen, the "Cassowary Lady." Tim and Theresa Leighton. Collin Livings. Save and Margaret Mostachetti. Eric Owen Camera Repairs. Peter Pavlov. Peter Schanco and his family. Karl and Mary Siener. Mr and Mrs Ron Stannart. Arthur and Margaret Thorsborne.

GABON: His Excellence Omar Bongo, President of Gabon, and the Ministers of Culture and National Education. Chief Doctor of the Republican Guard: Dr Mvou Yaloula Rigobert, and Nurse Michel Marie Aboui Bekalé. Dr Daniel-Boris Levi and his team at the Chambrier clinic. Mrs Basile. Madeleine and Bernard Boileau. Christian and Richard Cardoulis. Paula Chauvin. Pascal Chommeloux. Pierre Favier. Martine Shalimar-Feuillant. Denis Frère. Michel, Mireille and Samuel Gineste. The late Maurice and Micky Marion. Claude Marty and team. Jérôme, Isabelle, Léa and Alex Mathieu. Colette Mercier. Fifi Ndendé and Joseph. Clarisse Nguélé, from Ngounié. Michel "Pistol," Nina, Claude, the late Eric and Norbert Pradel from the Wongua-Wongué Presidential Reserve. Stéphane Prévost. Claude Rapy. Nadya Rekouche. Dr Malika and Jacques Saillans. SOBEA: Mr Jolibolis, N'Djolé sector. Mr Rodriguez. Robert and Michèle Sonnet. Mr and Mrs Suger. Jean Trolez. Monique Villeneuve and all those who contributed to the success of my expeditions during my various trips to Gabon. Logistic support, Mitsubishi (1988): Mr Petit, Freetown.

MADAGASCAR: The Minister of Animal Production, Water and Forests. Michel Alliotte Axel Aubry. Huguette Berger. Anita, Jean-Claude, Fred and Bruno Berger. Laurie Boswell, Lucien David. Mitou, Jean, Jo and Shupy Decampe. Chantal Gouet. Jean Lanoé. Jean-Marie and Yvonne Lebret. Xavier and Nathalie Metz. Jean Randresiarison. Claude Ranavirelo. Marcel Razafindrabe. Mr and Mrs Paul Razafy. Marceline Razanadrosoa. And everyone else...

INDONESIA: The Indonesian Embassy in Paris: Ambassador Dr Doddy A. Tisna Amidjaja, Minister Husni Thamrin and team, Mr Albert Anstein Purba and team. Mr Sutedja Kartawidjaja, Director of External Relations. The Ministry of Foreign Affairs. Mr Koski Zakaria, Director of Journalist Training. The Ministry of Information and Mr Ben B. Nadeak. Mr Ari Soodarsono, Director of the Department of Water and Forests and Mr Edi Susanto S.E.M. Aca. Sugandhy MSC, Ministry of Environment and Population. French Embassy in Jakarta: Alain Monteil and Francisca Pranoto, Philippe Alonso, Francis Maniel. Danny Parmady and Mr Bambam' Farm, Joseph Salvetti, Mrs Tantiens, Yosephina and Vince.

FRANCE: Dr Jean-Claude Andrault. Éliane Carrara. Claude Coquerelle. Jeannine De Cardaillac. Madeleine and Augustin Dumage. Fabienne Debwiller. Michel Felet. Jacques Geandaud. Marie-Claude and Hervé Lemée. Jean and Fiona Kay. Georges Lacroix. Micheline, Christine, Guillaume and Pascal Hersen. Museum of Natural History in Paris. Roger Bour. Raymond Pujol.

LOGISTIC SUPPORT AND SPONSORING
Air Madagascar: Mr Henri Roger. Antananarivo. Kodak-Pathé: Mr Sabatier, Mr Génin and Marie-Claude Perinelli. Kodak Great Reporting Grant. Several times winner of this grant, Nicole Viloteau has been using Kodak ektachrome 64 Asa and Kodachrome 64 Asa emulsion films since 1971, when her first photographs were published. Aspir (95110 Sannois, France), André Émerit venom pumps. Heaulme group hotels (Fort-Dauphin, Tuléar, Morondava) and Berenty Lemur Reserve. Decampe Hotels: Hotel Pangalanes (Tamatave). Garuda Airlines Indonesia (General Dr Fredie Maramis). The air company Garuda Indonesia greatly facilitated my transport to Indonesia, where I studied Komodo dragons and other reptiles on the island of Java.

CREDITS

PHOTOS: Page 178: Photo Delacotte/Viloteau, all rights reserved. Page 194: Photo Ed Elmer.
QUOTATIONS: Page 6, Charles Baudelaire, *Correspondences*, in *Selected Poems*. Trans. Joanna Richardson. Middlesex, England: Penguin Books, 1975. Page 10: Teilhard de Chardin, *Phénomène Humain*. Paris: Editions du Seuil, 1955. Page 58: Charles Darwin, *Voyage of the Beagle*. New York: Modern Library, 2001. Page 97: Antoine de Saint-Exupéry, *The Little Prince*. Trans. Katherine Woods. San Diego: Harcourt Brace, 1993. Page 128: William McFee, *The Market*, in Christopher Morley, *Modern Essays*. New York: Harcourt Brace, 1924. Page 142: *Dhammapada, The Sayings of Buddha*. Boston: Shambhala Pocket Classics, 1993. Page 194: Thomas Huxley, *A Liberal Education*, in *Collected Essays*. New York: Greenwood, 1968.

Translated from the French by Lisa Davidson. Copy-editing: Christine Schultz-Touge.
Color separation: Compos Juliot, Paris. Design: Caroline Chambeau. Typesetting: Studio X-Act, Paris.

Originally published as *Jungle Mystère* © 2000 Arthaud
English-language edition © 2001 Flammarion

ISBN 2-08010-662-8
FA0662-01-VII   Dépôt légal: 10/2001

Printed in Italy

CONTENTS

Dawn of the World 10

Immersion 22

Harmonious Geometry 42

Emerald Jewels 58

Jungle Mosaic 76

Dusk and Dawn 108

Bright Nights 128

Deadly Forest 142

Hide-and-Seek 162

Eyes of the Jungle 180

Yesterday and Tomorrow 194